Gentle Whisper
of the Secret Place
Adventures of a Hearing Heart

Gentle Whisper
of the Secret Place
Adventures of a Hearing Heart

Scott M. Holtz

Valrico, Florida

Unless otherwise indicated, all scriptural quotations are from the
New American Standard Bible, Copyright © 1960, 1962, 1963, 1968, 1971,
1972, 1973, 1975, 1977, 1995 by The Lockman Foundation.

Scripture verses marked KJV are taken from the *King James Version.*

Gentle Whisper of the Secret Place
Published by:
Flash Floods Publishing
P.O. Box 1799
Valrico, FL 33595-1799
www.flashfloods.com
ISBN 1-928536-00-X
Direct inquiries and/or orders to the above address.

Cover design and book production by:
DB & Associates Design Group,Inc.
dba Double Blessing Productions
P.O. Box 52756, Tulsa, OK 74152
www.dbassoc.org
Cover illustration is protected by the 1976 United States Copyright Act.
Copyright © 1999 by DB & Associates Design Group, Inc.

Printed in the United States of America.

Dedication

We dedicate this book to give the utmost resounding glory to our heavenly Father! Thank you for adopting us as your very own children and drawing us into your Secret Place. We love you Abba!

Contents

Contents

Acknowledgements

My joyful appreciation to all those who partnered with us in the Spirit and in financial support to bring this book to completion. Thanks to Michael and Sidra Murray for helping us gather and compile all the facts and testimonies. You all are tremendous blessings!

Foreword

This book is the story of Scott and Dalit Holtz' Holy Spirit adventures. They were a couple, once caught up in religion and tradition, Jewish believers bound by the rules and traditions of men. But then they had a visitation from God that changed their lives and their ministry. From this encounter, they embarked on the adventure of a lifetime. However, their story has only just begun. There is no telling what history will record of their lives.

From the first time I met them, I saw the hand of God upon them. I knew that God was going to use them in a unique way to touch the lives of countless numbers of people, who are crying out in the wilderness of life for the truth and for freedom.

The reason God is using them is because they will not compromise the truth of the Good News of the Gospel of the Lord Jesus Christ, the true Messiah. They are bold and obedient to do and say all that God requires of them. They acknowledge the third person of the Godhead — the Holy Spirit — in their lives and ministry and allow Him to have His way.

As their pastor, I would like to recommend Scott and Dalit's book to all of those trapped in religion and tradition. God wants you free! This is a challenge for you to step out of the boat and walk on the water of the supernatural with Scott and Dalit.

As you embark with them on a Holy Spirit, Book of Acts adventure, set in modern times — some of what you will read will seem incredible — but it is very real. I can vouch for their credibility and integrity. They are truly a blessing wherever they go. May you be both touched and challenged as you read their story.

— Dr. Rodney M. Howard-Browne
Revival Ministries International
Tampa, FL

In the past few years, ministers and ministries around the world have experienced an outpouring of the Holy Ghost characterized by an unspeakable joy, intoxication, and various signs and wonders. Some saw these manifestations as a phase or short-term experience. Others saw them as the result of a special anointing on a specific minister. Scott Holtz has recognized this as fresh outpouring of the Holy Spirit for all who are thirsty. Scott and his wife, Dalit, have been personally transformed by this outpouring. They have embraced the anointing and have become carriers of the awesome presence of God. They have ministered at Victory Fellowship several times, and always usher in a fresh outpouring of the glory of God. This book tells their story. Enjoy the *Gentle Whisper of the Secret Place*. Who knows, maybe you will find yourself caught up in the realms of God.

—Pastor Frank Bailey
Victory Fellowship
New Orleans, LA

I've known Scott and Dalit Holtz for a number of years and the one attribute that characterizes their life is a deep hunger for the move of God. I remember what

Jesus said about Nathaniel…Ah an Israelite, in whom there is no guile. In other words, what you see is what you get. Scott is like Nathaniel. No hidden agendas or motives. He just wants to see the Lord dramatically change and impact lives. I'm sure that is what you'll receive as you read this book.

—Evangelist Steve Solomon
Praise in the Night
Dallas, TX

Introduction

These pages you are about to read, meditate, and ponder on contain the story of two faceless messengers from simple backgrounds. Yet a deep hunger for the visitation of the glory of God upon our mission station in New York City caused us to press in and eventually discover the camouflaged entrance to the Secret Place of the Most High. Hemmed in on the outside by fierce persecution from the Ultra Orthodox Jewish community and a spiritual dryness from within, we discovered the still small voice of the Spirit of God and made ourselves available for specialized commando missions that initiated the plan of God in certain world events. These operations were all spontaneously birthed out of our extended revival meetings in local churches by the Holy Spirit's directive. All we endeavored to do was maintain a listening and yielded heart to step out in bold faith when He did His gentle bidding.

This is not just our story but the beginning of your story if you will also heed the message within these following pages with a hearing heart and then quickly rise up and just do whatever He tells you to do. Many of you have been given, throughout your Christian life, powerful prophetic words that still have not come to pass. Though you have treasured these promises within your heart, it seems as though they remain perpetually in a holding pattern of unfulfillment...just like the prophet Daniel in ancient Babylon, who read the former prophecy of

Jeremiah that the Jewish people would spend only 70 years in captivity then be released back to their own land. Daniel set his face in desperation to seek God and see the initiation of that prophetic word, since the 70 years were now completed. Daniel received more than what he had asked for and was even shown, not just the fulfillment of Jeremiah's prophecy, but also the apocalyptic 70 weeks and the coming of the Messiah, the future destruction of the Temple, and even the end days when communication and travel would explode on the world scene before the final resurrection of the dead (see Daniel 9-12).

In the same way, we can take the simple principles of God's Word and activate the promises of God in our lives by learning how to discover the still subterranean waters of the secret place. Time is short, and what must be done in this generation, must be done quickly. God is waiting on us to rise up and draw near to Him, and He will then draw near to us! The baton is in our hands. Will we pass it off to the next generation, or will we drive for the finish line?

We pray that the anointing that is upon our lives will thoroughly saturate and fill you as a wise virgin, so that you will fulfill your part in this great drama of the Glory of God unfolding on planet Earth in these last days. Be prepared as you read these pages for the Holy Spirit's gentle stillness to settle around your heart and mind and tell you also to "Arise and Shine" and do spontaneous operations in your neighborhoods and cities! Be bold and be strong, for this is the Church's finest hour!

In His glorious love,

Scott and Dalit Holtz

Rivers in the Desert International

...but the people that do know their God shall be strong, and do exploits   **Daniel 11:32 (KJV)**

Chapter 1
The Secret Place

After these things I looked, and behold, a door standing open in heaven, and the first voice which I had heard, like the sound of a trumpet speaking with me, said "Come up here, and I will show you what must take place after these things."

Revelation 4:1

"Come up here," he said.

Rodney Howard-Browne stopped his message and pointed to us. My wife, Dalit, and I left our seats and stood beside him in front of the crowd attending his 1993 Louisville Campmeeting.

"Who are you guys?" he asked.

"We pastor in New York City," I said. Immediately he began to prophesy over us. "The Jews need signs and wonders in New York City!"

Brother Rodney laid hands on us and we fell under the power of God. I lay on the floor saying, "Yes, this is it. This is it!" After twenty-six months of grueling work among the Russian Jews in Brooklyn, and constant persecution from Ultra-Orthodox Jews, we had come to campmeeting desperate for a refreshing from the Lord.

Brother Rodney continued ministering, stepping around Dalit who lay on the floor in front of the pulpit.

Four and a half-hours later she got up. Such glory radiated from her, I felt like I had a new wife!

"I've never seen anyone with such glory on them as I saw on your wife today," said Maurice Sklar, a gifted violinist. We talked for a while, then Maurice gave us a generous offering which we sorely needed. We'd driven from Brooklyn to the Louisville Campmeeting with only a hundred dollars in our pocket.

Strengthened and encouraged, Dalit and I returned to our Brooklyn apartment, and our children, Gideon and Deborah. Friends gathered around and we told them what had taken place in Louisville.

"Something's about to happen," we said. "Great signs and wonders are about to happen here among the Jewish people!" We believed a major revival would break out at any moment in the New York City metropolitan area, but ten months passed and no signs and wonders came.

However, *we* personally enjoyed the sweet fruit of revival; our newly tenderized hearts yielded more easily to God's will and to one another. Our marriage and the spirit in our home was transformed.

Meanwhile the pressures and frustrations of our ministry in Brooklyn only increased. Even so, we clung to God's unfulfilled prophetic words, becoming more and more hungry for a breakthrough into His fullness and purpose. Finally we reached a crisis point.

The Discovery

One day I got alone to meditate on the Scriptures. I turned to Hebrews 11:6 (KJV).

But without faith it is impossible to please him: for he that cometh to God must believe that he is, and that he is a rewarder of them that diligently seek him.

2

I read that promise and said, "Lord, I was touched powerfully by the anointing at Rodney's Campmeeting, and he prophesied over us. I was touched by the 1987 Arkansas River flash flood experience. Lord, aren't I diligently seeking you?"

I thought of all that we had been through in Brooklyn. My aching heart burst and I poured out my soul to God.

"Didn't we leave our friends in beautiful suburbia and move to Brooklyn, New York to preach the Gospel? Didn't you protect us from being driven out by the Ultra-Orthodox Jewish persecution? Don't I zealously study my Bible seeking to do your will so much that it's pages now look similar to a Dead Sea Scroll parchment from cave four at Qumran! We put our lives on the line to witness constantly in these streets with unique front line evangelistic outreaches. Wonderful things are happening in our ministry, but these prophetic words just seem to hang in the air, unfulfilled. Why aren't these things happening? Where's the beef!"

Again I looked at the text. "He is a rewarder..." I knew my Abba Daddy was a rewarder, not a penalizer. I ran a reference to Psalm 63 and there I noticed something for the first time.

I had been to the finest Bible schools, diligently studied the original languages and Biblical literature in graduate school, served in outreaches and short term missions and been mightily touched by the Holy Spirit in revival. I was certain I was diligently in hot pursuit of God, until I opened to Psalm 63:1 and found something I'd never seen nor heard before during 14 years of service to the Lord.

3

O GOD, You are my God; I shall seek You earnestly; My soul thirsts for You, my flesh yearns for You, In a dry and weary land where there is no water.

I immediately said, "Yes, that is exactly how I feel here in Brooklyn! In a dry spiritual wilderness just like the psalmist David!" I then quickly noticed a variation in the translation of the New American Standard Bible compared to the King James version of verse one which says, *O God, Thou art my God; **early** will I seek Thee....* I checked the Hebrew Masoretic text to see why the two translations differed, and discovered that the Hebrew word for "early" is the same Hebrew word describing seeking something "diligently and earnestly."

This is the ancient Hebrew verb *shahar* which means to seek something diligently as well as early. The parent noun form, *mishhar*, denotes the time just before sunrise or the dawn.[1] It is also a derivative word for a person with black hair in the Bible.[2] The Orthodox Jewish community still use this word *shaharit* to describe their early morning traditional prayer services. Suddenly it all came together.

In Hebrews 11:6, seeking Him diligently means not just going to Bible school, street witnessing, risking your life ministering in a hostile place. It also means getting up in the pre-dawn darkness, with an intense desire to fellowship with God. Scripturally, this is the ultimate way to seek God.

"Oh no," I said, "that's not what I wanted."

Then I considered how David wrote Psalm 63 while he lived in the wilderness of the Dead Sea region of Judah, hunted like a fugitive by King Saul. That's the most inhospitable place on earth, the same wilderness where Jesus fasted 40 days and faced and defeated Satan.

I decided I had to go for it, and resolved to get up before dawn and pray at our church.

The first morning I got up long before sunrise, drove over to the old synagogue that our congregation rented, and locked myself inside.

"Lord, we have had great revival services this last year but there's got to be more. I'm desperate for You. We need a breakthrough, Lord, right here in the spiritual wilderness of New York City!"

Off I went into my prayer language, interspersed with segments of English, praying through my laundry list of urgent prayer requests. When an hour of this religious exercise ended, I thanked the Lord and went on to my pastoral work for the day.

The second day I returned before dawn to the musty synagogue. I'd been through other early morning prayer programs, including a national ministry's teaching popular during the 1980's. I did as I'd been taught and commenced praying in the early morning blackness.

By the third day, I began dragging a little, my heavy eyelids blinking open and closing again. "Can't fall asleep," I told myself. "Come on!" I pressed on in prayer. By the fifth day the Energizer bunny slowed to a crawl. I knew that doing the same thing over and over while expecting different results is a sign of mental illness.

I admitted to myself that my prayers were only bouncing off the ceiling. We had experienced the river of revival, were pressed out for God ministering full time, and I was up praying at dawn. What more could I do?

"He who dwells in the secret place of the Most High shall abide under the shadow of the Almighty...I want that intimacy with you Abba! But where is it?"

Then I had a thought. "I'm too selfish, just praying for our own grocery lists of prayer requests. I've got to pray for the nations."

I jumped up and imagined a world map on the floor before me. I pointed towards the four corners of the world and interceded for the nations. I locked into a foreign sounding tongue and I pressed in with all my strength making myself agonize for the lost souls on planet earth. I thought to myself that this is real prayer discipline.

Day after day I kept coming to pray before the early morning dawn. If I found something in the Word, I pressed it to the limit, and this was no different. "He's a rewarder, not a penalizer," I kept telling my soul. Yet the heavens were shut up over me like brass.

The second week, running on pure desire and determination, I dragged myself into the building. On the second day of that week, utterly weary from these hours of praying in tongues and yelling with all my strength against the spiritual strongholds of New York City, all I could do was lay prostrate before the Lord. When I tried to pray my jaw muscles locked up in pain, refusing to function. I lay there before the Lord, stirring myself awake and drifting off again. God just let me wear myself out. Suddenly, in this place of despair and exhaustion the anointing flooded into me.

I jumped up being instantly revitalized by the anointing and began praying loudly in tongues again, but then the anointing drifted mysteriously away. I became still, and then the anointing returned. I started praying again out of rote and then the anointing lifted again. Finally I understood. Early morning praying = pain and fatigue. Early morning silence = anointing and refreshing. I do all the talking = no anointing and feels like religious jet lag. I shut up and be quiet = the waves of the anointing roll in and I experience the refreshing presence of Heaven.

The Lord wanted me to be *QUIET* before Him! He'd given me two ears and one mouth, so I needed to listen twice as much as I was talking during these first fruits of the day!

By the end of the second week, I was no longer in early morning prayer. God transformed my time before Him into early morning waiting, or tarrying. It was not something I had to enter in by doing desperate spiritual warfare, but rather worshipping Him and allowing His presence to settle in and around me during the early morning stillness. I began to understand that the Secret Place is not a geographical location, but it is a quiet positioning!

Look at Psalm 62:5. "My soul, wait in silence for God only, For my hope is from Him." How often do our congregations allow us to have silent, waiting meetings? Yet, Lamentations 3:26 states, "It is good that one should hope and wait silently for the salvation of the LORD."

Have you noticed during most worship services, when we come into a sweet silence, how often someone immediately has to rush into giving a tongue and an interpretation? Can't we just wait a while longer in His silent nearness? At home or in the car, are you so nervous about silence that you keep a TV, radio or tape playing? Do we want to hear from the Lord? Can we really hear what the Spirit is saying without first getting still before Him and listening for His voice?

When the prophet Elijah diligently sought after God and ran into the wilderness for fear of his life because of Jezebel's threatening rhetoric, he did not find God in the great wind rending the mountains and breaking in pieces the rocks, nor in the violent earthquake, nor in the blazing fire — but God was in the still, small voice. The Hebrew word describes that divine sound, *qol demama daqa,* as a small gentle whisper or the sound of a gentle blowing (1 Kings 19:12).[3]

This is alarming because Elijah, before this divine visitation in the wilderness and God's following rebuke, had already powerfully prophesied drought in all of Israel; supernaturally multiplied the provisions of the widow woman; and later raised her son from the dead; called fire down from Heaven on Mt. Carmel in the challenge against the prophets of Baal; prophesied the return of the rains; and the hand of the Lord came on him so that he outran the King's finest chariot and horses for many miles! He operated in all this power but still was not acquainted intimately with the gentle small voice! We must therefore take to heart the corresponding words of our Lord Jesus:

> **"Not everyone who says to Me, 'Lord, Lord,' will enter the kingdom of heaven; but he who does the will of My Father who is in heaven will enter.**
>
> **"Many will say to Me on that day, 'Lord, Lord, did we not prophesy in Your name, and in Your name cast out demons, and in Your name perform many miracles?**
>
> **"And then I will declare to them, 'I never knew you; depart from Me, you who practice lawlessness.'"**
>
> **Matthew 7:21-23**

Could it be that we can operate in powerful prophetic accuracy and amazing signs and wonders, and yet still not really know Him intimately? That knowing this still small voice is something many of us have not yet experienced and therefore keep doing what we think is right because the gifts of the Spirit are still manifesting in our lives and ministry. Then we categorically conclude we must be in God's perfect will because, after all, "Look at all that we are doing for the Kingdom of God!" In actual fact, if we are not watchful, we could be operating as a law unto ourselves even though great miracles are happening in our midst!

Unless the Lord builds the house, they labor in vain who build it; unless the Lord guards the city, the watchman keeps awake in vain.

It is vain for you to rise up early, to retire late, to eat the bread of painful labors; for He gives to His beloved even in his sleep.

Psalms 127:1,2

In this stillness before Him, I realized that if powerful signs and wonders are about to happen in our ministry, then I'd better get intimately acquainted with His still small voice, and not be disqualified later in this race of faith due to character problems like so many men and women of God that have gone before us. I also recognized during this time how my entire Christian life had been based on me talking, me praying, me doing this or that, rather than tarrying in silence before Him. The worship services of many of the North American churches I had attended were program and entertainment orientated to keep the attention of the people in the pews. I finally understood that He wanted me to study the Word and pray later in the day. But the first part of every morning was the time for Him to download His stillness into my spirit. And this is the ultimate pattern we are to follow of the Lord Jesus' devotional life in Mark 1:35.

In the early morning, while it was still dark, Jesus got up, left the house, and went away to a secluded place, and was praying there.

Consider these watershed events in the Bible that took place early in the morning. Abraham offered up Isaac on the altar (Genesis 22:3), Moses prophesied of the coming plagues to Pharaoh (Exodus 7:15; 8:20; 9:13), God looked out of the pillar of fire during the morning watch and destroyed the Egyptian army in the Red Sea (Exodus 14:24), Jesus rose gloriously from the dead (John 20:1-18), the Spirit was poured out mightily at the feast of Pentecost (Acts 2:1), Jesus Himself is known as "the Bright Morning Star"(Revelation 22:16), and He promises to give the bright morning star to every believer who overcomes (Revelation 2:28). To Him who has an ear, let him hear what the Spirit says to the churches!

By the third and fourth week of waiting on Him, God showed me the vital importance of getting a daily word from Him, fresh manna before the sunrise. *Man does not live by bread alone, but by every word that proceeds from the mouth of God.* We can't live on yesterday's manna. God wants us up early, with our satellite dishes open for a fresh download from heaven.

"I love those who love me; and those who diligently seek me will find me.

"Riches and honor are with me, enduring wealth and righteousness."

Proverbs 8:17,18

I also noticed during this time, that the above scriptural promise of Biblical prosperity (that had eluded my life up to this point in time), could also be found in the early morning blackness of intimate fellowship. Those who love Him and seek Him diligently/early (same Hebrew word "*shahar*" as in Psalms 63:1) are promised the weighty endowment of great riches and honor. Finally my search was over! The Holy Spirit's simple illumination of this one ancient Hebrew word became to me the hidden key that began to open up the elusive and camouflaged entrance to the secret place of the most High during this time of great desperation while in Brooklyn, New York! Glory to God! It was so simple!

Day by Day

So this became my routine. I'd get up before sunrise, while the kids were still asleep. Resisting the urge to hit the snooze button, I'd tell myself, "You snooze, you lose."

It was a fight with my groggy brain in a heavy body so early in the morning, but my spirit was always wide-awake, ready to soar. What a time to hear from Heaven, with so little static interference coming from my brain tissue!

I would begin behind locked doors with sincere thanksgiving and worship before the Lord until I sensed His sweet presence envelop me. Then I would wait in utter silence and reverent anticipation; my ear inclined to hear His gentle whisper. [Some have asked if I'm into Eastern meditation. No, I don't empty my mind...I *quiet* my mind and focus on Jesus the Messiah, basking in His pulsating presence, waiting for His voice of love and wisdom.] Most of the time I heard nothing, and I simply abode in His silence, beside the still waters.

When thoughts clamored for attention, beckoning me to do one thing or another, I would gently return my focus to Him. I learned to identify the three voices that came. First, there was the voice of my flesh, always complaining or restless with a list of things to hurry off and do. Second, there was the voice of my conscience, my spirit. And third, there was the sweet and gentle voice of the Holy Spirit. Only He knew Heaven's agenda for my day.

The Highest Level of Wisdom

God came to Solomon in a dream and said, "Ask! What shall I give you?" In 1 Kings 3:9, Solomon asked for *leb shome*.[4] This Hebrew word literally means, "a hearing heart." Solomon didn't ask for information or practical understanding, things we might associate with wisdom. Rather, he asked for a hearing heart. This is true biblical wisdom. God's Word goes forth continually, but the multitude of other voices often drowns Him out. That's why God did a sort of frontal lobotomy on me by hemming me into a crisis situation, and then letting me become speechless with fatigue before Him.

The Hebrew word *demama*,[5] refers to the still small voice Elijah heard in 1 Kings 19, and to the silence of Psalm 62, *My soul, wait in silence for God only....* Dalit was raised in Israel, so I asked her for the modern usage of this word. She said *demama* describes Israeli soldiers standing at attention, waiting to hear the command from their officer.

Another example occurs when Israel observes Holocaust Remembrance Day. At a set time, sirens blow, and the nation comes to a halt. Even traffic stops and everybody gets out of their cars and stands in the middle of the road. They bow their heads in silence and ponder what happened during the Holocaust. Israelis call this silent reflection, *demama*.

Sometimes we waited together, man and wife sitting in silent expectation before the Lord. At other times a few others joined us in those early hours. Those first weeks were hard, but I knew Abba would come through. Our part was to believe and obey.

There are many other Scriptural references to our being silent before God. Habakkuk 2:20 is an example. But the *LORD is in His holy temple, Let all the earth be silent before Him.* The margin of my NASB reads this verse "Hush before Him, all the earth." This idea of being caught up in His tranquil quietness is found also in Psalm 23:2, "still waters, or waters of rest," Psalm 46:10, "Be still and know that I am God; I will be exalted among the nations, I will be exalted in the earth." The margin of my NASB also reads uniquely this verse as "Let go, relax!" Praise God, I was now starting to like this relaxing part since I was trained to always be so busy doing something for the Kingdom of God! The thought of relaxing and letting go was altogether a new prayer discipline — one I could really enjoy!

Divine Appointment

Tired of sticking my nose in the fetid carpet of the old synagogue, I decided to meet with Abba out on Coney Island beach. Ignoring the broken wine bottles, drug syringes and other litter of a dying society, I sat at dawn before the open water and pure sunlight. I sang to Him, whose glory will soon cover the earth as the waters cover the sea, and I waited for His will.

One morning, I felt His gentle Presence pulsating over me. Captivated by my Lord, I wanted nothing but to be caught up with Him. When it came time to leave, I drove home along the Belt Parkway with New York City's rush hour traffic gathering momentum.

Just up ahead, a car cut into traffic and ran down a man on a motorcycle. I pulled over and leapt out. The driver, a Russian woman, stood shrieking above a Jamaican man pinned against his bike in a spreading pool of gasoline.

Rubbernecking motorists nearly collided, horns blared around us, and sirens demanded a path through the traffic. I knelt down and lifted the man's head out of the gasoline.

"Don't touch him," I thought. "He could have AIDS!"

Yet, the compassion of Jesus flooded my heart, driving out all fear. With internal injuries draining his strength, the man's trembling hands stuffed little bags of crack cocaine down his throat. I rebuked the spirit of death, and prayed with this soul who lingered on the edge of the abyss. With faint hope, the man stared up at me, his brown eyes glazing over in shock.

Paramedics shoved me aside, jostled the man onto a gurney and hauled him away. I got back into my car and sat there with gasoline fumes burning my nostrils. Waves of weeping and joy swept over me.

"Yes Lord," I cried out. This is what life on this planet is all about. I'll do this every day. Put me one meter from the gates of hell and let me rescue prisoners about to fall into the eternal flames of Hell!"

And I heard the Lord gently say, *"Son, if you hadn't come before me early this morning, I could not have positioned you later in the morning to rescue that man."*

Then it became clear to me. Early morning waiting allows the Holy Spirit to download into me fresh anointings for the people and situations I'll meet that day. Then I'm led from one divine appointment to another, like falling dominos, bringing His fresh impartation to hungry and hurting people.

Beginning our day in the Secret Place lifts us into a flow of Christ's divine purposes. Suppose you had obeyed Jesus the last time He woke you at four in the morning...what might Abba Father have done through you that day? What works of gold and silver have you traded for more sleep?

The Breakthrough

On June 10, 1994, during the sixth week of early morning waiting, I returned to the old synagogue and silenced myself before the Lord. First light reached in through a sooty window. And just then God's glory flooded my inner man with light. Often we look for the spectacular and miss the supernatural, but this morning I did not miss it, praise God! I found myself again in the place called *"there."* Abba drew me into His bosom and surrounded me with His love. Like the gentle rustling of the leaves, He whispered into my hearing heart. Years before I had clearly heard His voice, but in the Secret Place, I rediscovered His voice in deep stillness.

"Son, I want you to take your wife and a few others, go stand in front of the places in New York City that are offensive to Me, and blow the shofar for judgment." The Lord said.

I heard His commission with absolute clarity. I knew that we were entering into a different anointing and that something new was now being fulfilled in our lives. Thrilling joy surged through me. The prophetic word over us at the 1993 Louisville Campmeeting was now erupting. I had finally discovered how to activate the promises of God through the still subterranean waters of the Secret Place!

Maybe you're thinking, "Wow, six weeks. I can't make it." But you have to make it. Fulfilling His purposes for your life depends on it. And it may not take you six weeks. For one thing, you don't have to go through the weeks of vain repetition as I did before finally quieting myself before Him. It all depends on your hunger for change and your willingness to cease from your own works and yield to His still small voice. It's your choice: more of the status quo, or break through into the Secret Place of the Most High? If you can't run with the footmen today, what will you do when the horsemen gallop onto the world scene?

Shofar Exploit

The following evening, preparing to go out and blow the shofar, I felt like a Cruise missile being launched for multiple detonations on unknown enemy targets.

"This feels like a commando raid," I said to Dalit and several friends gathered in our Brooklyn apartment. The looks on their faces showed the heightened anticipation we felt. A friend from my days at Oral Roberts University, Tom Nicholson, had suddenly canceled revival meetings in Maryland and come to visit that weekend. We were joined by Don and Lisa Geraci, Assembly of God ministers.

We walked out into the humid evening of Saturday, June 11, 1994. I drove with Tom and Dalit, while the Geracis followed us over to the Crown Heights section of Brooklyn.

It is the wisdom and mercy of God that we often obey Him without a full understanding of what we're doing. Though we couldn't have imagined what was about to happen, I silently told the Lord my reservations about the target of our mission.

"Lord, you're sending us to the headquarters of the same people who have ruthlessly opposed us for two years." I reminded the Lord of my tender age and lack of life insurance. But there was no turning back.

The first place I sensed the Spirit leading us to blow the shofar for judgment was at the Lubavitch World Headquarters. The power of this radical, Ultra-Orthodox Jewish sect reached around the world, led by an extraordinary rabbi named Menachem Mendel Schneerson. Tens of thousands of his followers were pressing forward with their plans to soon crown him Messiah. Tom sat beside me, the shofar across his lap. I found Dalit's face in the rearview mirror.

Reggae music throbbed from an open market brightly painted sky blue and mango orange. We had crossed into the Caribbean neighborhood. The low sun slanted through the smog into crowds gathered on the sidewalk. Shadowed faces peered from ramshackle buildings. A well-groomed Jamaican family passed through a dope-smoking crowd of Rastafarians. A few blocks later, we crossed into the Ultra-Orthodox neighborhood. It might as well have been another country.

Tensions smoldered between the two enclaves since August 1991, when Rabbi Schneerson returned from visiting his wife's grave in Queens, and someone in the motorcade ran over a seven year-old black boy, killing him. His accidental death ignited the infamous Crown Heights riots.

We turned the corner onto the seven hundred block of Eastern Parkway. Blue patrol cars of the New York City Police Department waited at positions strategic to the red brick, Lubavitch World Headquarters, their synagogue and the private home of Rabbi Schneerson. Uniformed and plainclothes officers stood guard against another terrorist attack.

The Gulf War was over, officially at least. But not long ago a Palestinian man had opened fire on a Lubavitch school bus, killing and wounding several Yeshiva students.

Close to 7 p.m. the Lubavitchers were gathering to begin their prayers, ending the Shabbat, the Sabbath. Thousands of bearded men and their sons emerged from the surrounding homes and synagogues into the streets. Most were dressed in their usual black hats and black suits over white shirts, but some wore long black garments and round-brimmed hats edged with fur. The women and girls remain segregated both inside the synagogues and out on the streets. During this time before the end of Shabbat, the Lubavitchers mingle along the streets and sidewalks.

World Wide Lubavitch

It's difficult for an outsider to grasp the influence and power of Rabbi Schneerson and the Lubavitcher movement that he's headed since 1950. He was born in 1902 in the Ukraine, the son of a renowned Kabbalist and Talmudic scholar. A child prodigy in Torah study, Schneerson grew up to become the seventh in a dynastic line of leaders of the movement founded during the 18th century. With his magnetic personality and piercing blue eyes, Schneerson gathered to himself the undivided devotion of hundreds of thousands, perhaps millions of followers.

Under his leadership, they opened full-time yeshivas for Jewish men and women with little or no background in Torah study. Schneerson was the inspiration and driving force behind a revitalized outreach program that affected the full spectrum of Jewish life.

Typical of his ideas were the so-called "mitzvah mobiles." They parked these vans around New York, offering passers-by a convenient opportunity to come in and do "mitzvah" (fulfilling a commandment) on the spot, such as taking home Shabbat candles or putting on "tefillin" (leather prayer straps). The rebbe called them "Jewish tanks to combat assimilation."

He advocated outreach to deprived Jewish children and to isolated Jews on campuses or living under repressive regimes all over the world. The rebbe led a constant expansion of far-flung Lubavitch communities from the

American Midwest to the Pacific Rim and from Australia to the former Soviet Union.

Though his words were often broadcast to the Lubavitch network by phone or satellite hookup, he rarely left Brooklyn and had never visited Israel. An exact replica of his Brooklyn home was nearly completed in Israel, preparing for his move to the land and finally the proclamation of Rabbi Schneerson as the "Moshiah" or Messiah.

Before he suffered a stroke, huge crowds lined up every Sunday waiting their turn to file into Schneerson's house and stand face to face with the great man. He blessed each one and gave them a crisp dollar bill to be donated to the charity of their choice.

Jewish organizational leaders, many of them not religious, sought out Schneerson's advice and special blessing on important projects. Every day, sacks of mail arrived from followers, many of whom would not take a new job or marry without first seeking his council. All over the world, his followers hung his picture in their homes and even their offices. But his power and influence reached far beyond religion, exerting a profound influence on local politics all the way to Israel.

During the Gulf War, when scuds rained down on Israel, Yitzak Shamir ordered missiles tipped with nuclear weapons readied for launch. At that critical hour, many in Israel looked to Schneerson for direction. He advised them not to retaliate; assuring them the enemy would soon be defeated. Israel stayed her nuclear hand, and the immediate and overwhelming Allied victory proved Schneerson right. He wielded such political influence in Israel that his support during elections determined the outcome between Likud and Labor.

The New York Daily News reported that in 43 years, Schneerson built the once obscure movement into a political and financial powerhouse. He became the most influential Jewish religious leader in the world, with over 200,000 followers in 130 countries and controlled $500 million in Lubavitch holdings.[6] Many leaders, both within and outside the movement, described Rabbi Schneerson as the foremost Jewish personality of modern times.

According to Jewish tradition, there's a potential messiah in every generation who will reveal himself when and if the world is ready. Many Lubavitchers were convinced "the rebbe" was that Messiah, and they began setting the stage to crown him Moshiah.

In the late 1970's they launched a massive campaign to recapture intense, messianic faith from the Gentiles.

The slogan, "We Want Moshiah (Messiah) Now," became the rallying cry for this multi-million dollar international media campaign. While many followers showered Schneerson with adoration, most activists at that time dismissed claims that their rebbe was the Messiah. However, in 1992 Lubavitchers launched their "Prepare for the Coming of the Messiah," campaign, with that slogan appearing everywhere on bumper stickers and billboards.

Though Schneerson never openly claimed to be the Messiah, he did move in supernatural powers. Barren women conceived after receiving his blessing, many claimed miraculous healings and pointed to extraordinary blessings and solutions to difficult problems resulting from the rebbe's powers.

In 1992, Rabbi Schneerson suffered a stroke, leaving him immobilized and unable to communicate. His inner circle rushed to fill the power vacuum, but in his absence, conflict arose over the course of the movement. Their main disagreement centered around the campaign to declare Schneerson the Messiah. Even his stroke and protracted illness were interpreted in messianic terms. They pointed to the suffering Messiah verses in Isaiah 53, and claimed Schneerson was suffering for the sins of the Jewish people. It was during this time of heightened expectation that the campaign "King Moshiah" had finally begun.

Day of Reckoning

I knew if we rolled past the headquarters and stuck a long shofar out the window, the police might mistake us for drive-by shooters and open fire. I decided to have Tom blow the shofar from a block away, thereby avoiding both the police and the likelihood of physical aggression by the Lubavitch men crowding the street around us.

"No," said Dalit. "You're going to blow the shofar right in front of their door!" Facing this ex-Drill Sergeant from the Israeli Army, I realized that she was right.

"OK, let's go."

We drove forward and rolled to a stop outside the front door. Tom lifted the Yemenite shofar to his lips. TRHhuaAH! TRHhuaAH! His soaring blasts flew against the brick buildings and echoed on the evening air. The crowd seemed to stand still, stunned by the wailing notes of the ancient trumpet.

"Why are these Gentiles blowing the shofar?" they asked one another in Yiddish and Hebrew. The Spirit fell upon Dalit, and she cried out to them.

"Rend your hearts and not your garments!"

She turned to me and asked, "What does the word rend mean?" Dalit speaks fluent Russian and Hebrew.

English is her third language and she didn't know what she had prophesied.

"Schneerson's a nabi shequer!" I cried. "Schneerson's a false prophet. Jesus is the Messiah!"

The Spirit gripped me with His love for these Jewish people, disciplined scholars who are zealous for God but without understanding, unable to see through the veil shrouding rabbinical Judaism.

"Return O Israel," I pleaded. "Why will you die, O house of Israel?"

We expected the staring crowd to spew blasphemous words against the Lord Jesus. But they were mysteriously quiet. The light turned green and we rolled forward, carefully making our way through the crowd of black suits and white faces.

The police lifted their barricades from the neighborhood streets where no traffic passes from Friday evening to Saturday evening, in honor of Shabbat. Our car was one of the first to drive down the quiet streets, so the Lubavitchers strolling home heard our Gospel message as we passed them.

Next I sensed the Spirit leading us to drive to the major synagogues of Brooklyn. I knew all their locations, so off we went. For hours we drove around, worshipping God and stopping to blow the shofar and proclaim the Gospel outside Brooklyn's important synagogues. At 10:30 p.m. we returned to our apartment, enjoying a clear sense of the Father's approval. After praying, we said goodnight and went to sleep.

Sunday morning we relaxed at home with our guest. Tom wanted to buy some Judaic gifts, so I phoned a local religious store to see if they were open yet. A woman answered.

"We are closed," she said. "Don't you know?"

"Know what?"

"What? Already all Brooklyn knows of this tragic event. Rabbi Schneerson died suddenly last night!"

Stunned, I said good-bye and hung up the phone.

"What's wrong?"

"Schneerson died last night!"

"What? He's dead?"

We did not rejoice over the rebbe's death. Though he was a blind leader of the blind, there's never joy in the passing of any soul without the grace of God.

Tom and I hurried out, leaving Dalit to make arrangements for the children and follow us later. Driving toward the Lubavitch Headquarters, we listened to news bulletins on the radio and heard them describing the sudden passing of Rabbi Schneerson beginning at 7 p.m. last night.

[The newspapers later confirmed what we were hearing on the radio and reported that the beloved 92-year-old spiritual leader had died Sunday morning at 1:50 a.m. at Beth Israel Medical Center, where he had been on a respirator since a stroke in March; and that according to hospital officials, he went into cardiac arrest at 7 p.m. Saturday.[7]]

This was the exact time we blew the shofar.

Tom and I looked at one another, hardly comprehending what had happened. Further reports detailed how thousands of mourners, including national figures, were flying in from around the world. One report told how, shortly after Schneerson's last breath, a siren cried out from Lubavitch Headquarters and the news quickly spread around the world.

Two signals were sounded from the same place that fateful night. At Sabbath's end, our shofar signaled judgment and across town in a hospital, the rebbe's heart faltered. Seven hours later, the Lubavitch siren wailed in the night, declaring his death.

Ironically, in the pre-dawn darkness, the New York Daily News reported that hundreds had gathered along Eastern Parkway weeping and praying during their own early morning *shaharit* ritual. Yet others came singing, drinking Budweiser and pounding tambourines as they danced! One young reveler was reported to have said that the rebbe taught them that when they dance and sing it adds life force to the rebbe himself; and that Schneerson had guaranteed them that *he is* the Messiah. So they were celebrating the holiday of redemption... how could they be sad?"[8]

This weeping over the death of their rebbe by some, and the celebration of his soon resurrection by others, is typical of the schism dividing the movement to this day.

None of the radio reports prepared us for the scene at Lubavitch Headquarters, that Sunday morning.

A Sea of Black

We parked and walked through the very neighborhood where my father had lived as a little boy until his parents moved to avoid the Ultra-Orthodox influx. Everywhere around us now, people wearing black hurried toward the same place. Police estimated that more than 50,000 followers and friends of Rabbi Schneerson gathered outside his home. Mourners greatly outnumbered dancers among the throng jammed along the streets and sidewalks around the Headquarters.[9]

We found ourselves swept into a line winding through the surging, wailing mass of Hassidim and filing into the rebbe's house. So we decided to go inside and see for ourselves.

24

Dignitaries waited their turn in line. Standing behind me was a delegate from President Clinton, and Colette Avital, Israel's UN Consul General. New York's Mayor Rudolph Guiliani paid his respects, along with Benjamin Netanyahu, then leader of Israel's opposition Likud bloc.

While all this was happening in New York, over in Israel crowds of Lubavitcher Hassidim were packed into Ben Gurion International Airport trying to buy *any* ticket that would get them to the funeral. None of the airlines had adequate accommodations for the massive crowds at the airport, even though El Al Israel Airline did schedule a jumbo jet for at least 450 followers.[10]

When our turn came, Tom and I stepped out of the sunlight, across the threshold and into the dim residence. Hopeless grief shrouded the old house. Plainclothes security men and New York City Police stood watch over the mourners shuffling past the open doorway of the rebbe's study. The Orthodox man in front of me looked into the study, moaned and went to pieces.

I stepped forward and looked to my right into the book-lined study. The rebbe's small body lay on a gurney, covered with a white sheet. Ashen-faced rabbis with long white hair and beards, swayed up and down, murmuring desperate prayers for Schneerson to rise from the dead. My spirit recoiled from the presence of darkness pervading the scene.

"He's not getting up," we said. "He's dead!"

Security men grabbed us and ushered us back outside, right into the lights of New York's WPIX TV. Cameras from CNN and news bureaus from around the world covered the spectacle.

"One blast from the shofar," I said to Tom, "and the whole world's here watching!"

25

*Coffin of Grand Rebbe Menachem Schneerson
is carried out of Lubevitcher Headquarters at the same location the shofar was
sounded the evening before*

A Lubavitch spokesman faced the TV camera in front of me. "With the rebbe now dead," said the reporter, "who will be his successor?"

"There's no successor," said the spokesman. "He is our Messiah."

"Excuse me," I said, leaning toward the camera. "There is no successor. Jesus is the Messiah!"

Like Stephen in the midst of the Sanhedrin, I felt the gnashing of teeth from the Ultra-Orthodox surrounding us. I knew we could be attacked right then, so powerful is the spirit of antichrist animating these misguided Lubavitchers. Yet somehow, we walked untouched through their midst.

For hours, Tom and I stayed at the scene, witnessing as we could. When late shadows stretched over the grieving throng, Dalit arrived. She stood among thousands of Ultra-Orthodox women and schoolgirls pressed behind police barriers. Inside the house, the leaders gave up trying to raise their messiah from the dead, and carried the rebbe's body out in a pine box. A haunting, hopeless wail filled the streets.

"Our king. Our teacher. Our messiah, don't leave us," they screamed!

Dalit said their grieving was like that of Zechariah 12, when one day the Jewish people...*will look on Me whom they pierced. Yes, they will mourn for Him as one mourns for his only son....* Fierce with grief, many of them took out knives and scissors and cut and tore their clothing according to tradition. We watched them rending their garments at the exact place on the sidewalk where, the evening before, Dalit prophesied from Joel 2,...*rend your heart and not your garments!*

God had sent us to the world headquarters of rabbinic power and the most significant false messianic

*Many Lubavitchers believe he will raise from the dead
and declare himself the Messiah*

figure of the last twenty centuries of Jewish Common Era history. There we sounded the alarm, proclaimed Jesus Lord and Schneerson a false messiah, then prophesied that they must repent and rend their hearts. God confirmed His warning to them by striking their leader's heart, even as the shofar sounded. Their refusal to repent was now complete.

In the midst of this awesome display of His sovereign purpose, the Spirit spoke to me again. After my breakthrough into the Secret Place, my ear was now more attuned to His gentle whisper.

"You have obeyed Me by bringing the gospel to the Jew first, according to Romans 1:16. You blew the shofar of warning at this false messiah's headquarters. Most of them did not listen. Now I am sending you to blow the second trumpet into My Church."

28

Joel 2 speaks of a first and a second trumpet. The first trumpet, in verse one, is an alarm on the holy mountain. *...Let all the inhabitants of the land tremble, for the day of the LORD is coming....* The fifteenth verse speaks of a second trumpet. *"Blow a trumpet in Zion, consecrate a fast, proclaim a solemn assembly....* This leads to verse 18,19, and 28.

Then the LORD will be zealous for His land and will have pity on His people.

The LORD will answer and say to His people, "Behold, I am going to send you grain, new wine, and oil, and you will be satisfied in full with them; and I will never again make you a reproach among the nations.

"It will come about after this that I will pour out My Spirit on all mankind...."

That word from the Lord launched us into our present ministry. We travel throughout the nations strengthening the Church and sounding the second trumpet calling God's people to solemn assemblies, which are really extended revival meetings. Under the anointing in His awesome presence, people rend their hearts in repentance. Then the Holy Spirit ignites their cleansed hearts with intoxicating joy and revived fervency for Jesus.

For You

I'm writing this book so you won't waste years as I did, pursuing knowledge in seminary at the expense of intimacy with God. Look steadfastly at Jesus. He never let His agenda be dictated by the insatiable human needs pressing around Him. He only said what He heard the Father saying. He only did what He saw the Father doing. Jesus never became preoccupied with ministry and neglected hearing Abba's gentle whisper in the Secret Place.

All this came to us through a hunger for God, which drove us into a solitary experience with Him in the early morning hours. By His grace, we tapped into His subterranean rivers in our hearts, a downloading channel direct from Abba's heart. Now He sends us out on Holy Ghost Rambo missions, to exhort the true Body of Messiah to fill their lamps with oil before the Bridegroom's soon return.

Be warned, dear friend, only one thing separated the five wise virgins from the five foolish ones. All ten were virgins and all ten slumbered until the midnight cry. All ten had lamps burning with the gospel light, and all ten trimmed their lamps and went out to meet the bridegroom. But only the wise virgins had extra oil in their vessels. And only the wise virgins went in with the bridegroom to the wedding.

Olive oil for their lamps was produced at the olive press. The word "Gethsemane" is the Aramaic word for the olive press.[11] And it was there in that garden that our Bridegroom yielded. "Abba, not my will, but Thine be done." The wise virgins are those who have been pressed by His Spirit to press in and know Him intimately as Abba, Daddy, and not just as Lord. Their hearing hearts have become yielded to His will and not their own and therefore have enough oil to be known by Him and enter the wedding feast.

Chapter 2
From Tulsa and Leningrad

"...remove your sandals from your feet, for the place on which you are standing is holy ground."

Exodus 3:5

The awesome voice filled the darkened movie theater where I sat beside my father, watching "The Ten Commandments." While the burning bush scene lit up the wide screen, a tangible presence gripped me with awe and wonder. As the young son of an unbelieving Jewish father, I'd not even heard of the Holy Spirit. But I never forgot how that powerful presence came upon me.

I grew up in Tulsa, Oklahoma. My father was a prosperous trial attorney. My Irish mother had accepted Judaism, but we ignored our religion except for a few Jewish traditions. The synagogue where I studied for my Bar Mitzvah zealously indoctrinated us against the Gospel. One day, walking down the hall of the synagogue, I stopped. There stood a large bronze sculpture of the burning bush.

A question sparked my soul. "How could a bush be on fire and not be burned up?" I wondered. The holy presence of His stillness came upon me again, the same presence I had experienced years earlier in the movie theater. I neither understood it nor spoke of it to

31

anyone, and passed my high school years in the usual pursuits of a godless, suburban teenager.

In 1979, Missouri Southern State College recruited me to play goalie for their nationally ranked soccer team. My father wanted me to follow him to the Ivy League, but soccer was my passion. During the Fall semester I played goalie and reveled in the party scene, hardly bothering with classes.

On the night of December 9, I staggered into my dorm room drunk on whiskey and beer. My first semester grade point average was .9; and in a few days I would face my parents at Winter break. I flopped on my bed, and sat there with my head spinning. Two football players walked in, one a Charismatic Catholic and the other a Spirit-filled Baptist. I recognized the unseen presence of a Third Person entering with them. The running back was training the huge offensive lineman how to win souls with *The Four Spiritual Laws* tract. The lineman's beefy fingers mistakenly turned the pages of the little tract directly to step number three.

"Hey what're you doing?" said the running back. "He's a sinner. You have to read number one and two before number three!"

Their lack of technique didn't matter. The Holy Spirit seized me with such love and conviction that I couldn't even look at the two guys. I kept telling them I was Jewish and they kept telling me the Gospel.

"Scott, do you want to pray the prayer of salvation?"

"Yes," I said. And when I prayed, "Jesus, come into my heart and forgive me of my sins," I saw a black cloud leave my body. My mind cleared. I looked at them now sober and delivered.

"Wow! What happened to you?"

"I feel great," I said. They jumped up and ran down the hall, telling others what God had just done for me. With my conscience clean and pure for the first time in my life, I lay down and fell into a deep, sweet sleep.

The next evening, I walked into a dorm room Bible study that was packed with more than thirty athletes. I sat in the back, my long hair and Budweiser T-shirt isolating me among the clean-cut crowd. All around me guys huddled and talked with such excited expectation that I felt afraid.

"Who wants to receive the Holy Ghost?"

"It's Jesus!" I gulped. The assistant basketball coach suddenly stood before us. With his beard, white robe and sandals, he had startled me momentarily into thinking he was Jesus.

"What's the Holy Ghost?" I wondered.

"I've been fasting for two weeks," the coach said. "The Lord showed me this revival needs to go to the next level."

I didn't know it yet, but I'd been born again into the midst of a full-blown campus revival, led by this coach. He opened to the Gospel of Mark and began teaching on the Baptism of the Holy Spirit. A mammoth lineman named Gomer, stirred himself and raised his great frame to full height beside me.

"That ain't from God," said Gomer. "That stuff went out with the last apostle!" The coach kept teaching and Gomer kept arguing. Later, the coach laid hands on the dorm's Resident Assistant and this Southern Baptist began laughing and weeping and speaking in unknown languages. Stunned, I sat there wondering what in the world was happening.

All around the room, guys broke into joy and weeping and euphoric worship. The coach prayed for one after another, and the Baptizer filled them with His Spirit and they spoke in other tongues. Just then a glimmer caught my right eye. I turned and saw a misty light coming through the window. The golden haze hovered a few feet from me, filling the upper part of the room with a smoky brilliance.

No one else seemed to see this shimmering mist that pulsed in and out of view. I stared transfixed, watching those who raised their hands into the hovering presence immediately receive the Spirit and break into tongues with tears and laughter. The Shekinah glory cloud moved over Gomer.

He cried out in an unknown tongue. Then he said, "I don't believe in this!" Back and forth went Gomer, stammering his doctrinal position in English then laughing and crying and speaking in tongues. Everybody burst into ecstatic praise and worship. I grabbed my jacket and bolted from the room. Clank went the exit bar as I threw open the outside door and sprinted into the winter night. Frigid air filled my lungs as I ran through the darkness, far into a hayfield. Catching my breath, I looked around to be sure I was alone. Then I lifted my eyes toward the clear sky and spoke aloud.

"God, I'm going home in a few days. If I tell my parents I believe in Jesus I know what they'll say. God I'm so confused...*Baruch Atah Adonai Elohaynu Melek*...Oh, what was that prayer?"

I couldn't recall the Hebrew prayers I'd learned for my Bar Mitzvah. The presence I'd felt minutes before now descended upon me. Something bubbled within me like rapid bursts of power. Fluent Hebrew rolled off my tongue. The holy presence swirled around me and I sensed divine understanding blow into my spirit.

In perfect English I spoke aloud the interpretation of the Hebrew tongue.

"I am the God of your fathers, Abraham, Isaac and Jacob. I sent my Son to die for the sins of the whole world and for your sins."

"But, how can that be? How can that be?" I cried. Confusion gripped my mind, but my heart knew the truth. I recognized the presence of this invisible Person, and recalled the other past times He had visited me sitting in the movie the "Ten Commandments" with my father and later standing in the synagogue before the sculpture of the burning bush.

The Lord continued, saying, *"I am going to send you to the Jewish people."*

The dark field lit up with that same golden mist. Like Moses who made haste to worship God, I threw myself face down on the frozen ground, shaking in the fear of the Lord. More interpretation of the Hebrew continued, but now there was an added dimension.

While speaking out in English I saw in my spirit the same things I heard myself describing. I glimpsed my future wife, our family and our ministry to Israel and the nations. The light blazed up in dazzling splendor, suspending me in that timeless realm. The next morning I woke up in my dorm bed still under the strong hand of His anointing and with a brand new faith-filled relationship with God. I'd been kidnapped by His glory.

That encounter birthed in me a hunger to know God's heart and to please Abba Father. To be in His glory realm became the driving force of my life.

At Winter break I went home. I found my mother agonizing with a ruptured disc in her spine.

"What happened to your face?" she said, seeing the glowing change in my countenance.

"I met Jesus."

"You what?" She sat down. "Oh, my back's killing me!"

"Mom, listen. I read in the Gospels where it's all in red ink. Jesus says we can lay hands on the sick and they'll be healed."

"Oh," she said, "anything for this pain."

While my little brother and sister watched Gilligan's Island on TV beside us, I reached out to my mother and touched her back.

"Jesus, You can do this!" She was shocked as God's healing power restored her back.

"Oh wow, wait 'till I tell Dad!" I said.

"Now wait a minute, honey. You know your father." When my father got home I hurried to greet him. He was so glad to see me. "Dad, something incredible happened to me," I said. "I met the Lord Jesus. And He healed mom!" "You did what?" He roared at me! Later I was asked to leave the house.

This may sound harsh, but some Jews actually hold funeral services for their children who come to Jesus. I piled all my clothes into my pickup truck and drove away. I phoned my buddies at the revival and told them how my father had kicked me out of the house.

"Wow that is awesome! Praise God!" they said. "Persecution means a bigger crown you know! Now you need to find a good church."

During winter break, I stayed with a friend in Tulsa and went looking for a place to worship. In my final attempt to find God in my rabbinic heritage, I went that Friday night to our temple. I sat down and Rabbi Rosenthal kept eyeing me as he taught the congregation.

My spirit probed for God's presence, but He was not there in the synagogue. I got up and walked out.

In the area was a Roman Catholic church. I walked up to the door and stepped over the threshold of a place I'd been warned never to enter. I looked around the dim deserted church.

"Oh!" I gasped, startled by a life-sized marble saint staring from beyond flickering candles. The old pew creaked as I sat down in the eerie quiet. I waited but no one came, so I hurried out.

I drove and found a Methodist church, and I went inside. I felt a little better in there, but I wondered what sort of ceremony was going on. The minister appeared beside me and spoke softly.

"Young man, we're having a most wonderful foot washing. The Holy Spirit is here!" "Really?" I said to myself. "I don't recognize His presence in here like it was in that field." So I headed for the door. Later I visited a large, Spirit-filled church, where five meetings every Sunday were needed to serve the thousands drawn to the dynamic ministry. I knew nothing of doctrines or programs, but that church passed my inner man's litmus test for having the same presence of the glory of God I had experienced in the Missouri hayfield as when I'd visited their worship services.

What Faith Is

I returned to the Missouri campus for the 1980 Spring Semester and found myself in the midst of revival. The Baptist Student Union effectively became the Pentecostal Student Union. I'm thankful I was born again into revival rather than being ushered into some local denomination where I'd have traded my old shackles for religious bondage.

During the summer term I moved into an apartment with two brothers in the Lord, Randy and Mark. We covenanted together to spur one another on in our walk, agreeing to abstain from ungodly TV and the Christian dating scene. One night the three of us piled into my Silverado and rode over to the outskirts of Joplin, Missouri.

We drove onto the deserted lands of an abandoned lead mine, rolling past huge black mounds of mining chaff hunched in the darkness. We got out. Mark grabbed his guitar and we climbed into the back of my pickup truck and sat down.

We settled into the warm stillness beneath a magnificent, starry sky. The song of the crickets seemed to grow louder the longer we watched the shooting stars burn across the heavens. Mark played his guitar and we sang to the One who spoke the Word and galaxies whirled into being. Suddenly Mark stopped playing, looked up and spoke a simple prayer.

"Jesus, give us a sign of Your soon return."

He resumed playing and we lifted our voices, "Hallelujah, Hallelujah..." "Look at that!" I said.

We watched a brilliant light fly over the horizon from the northeast, coming toward us. I thought it must be a low-flying jet with its landing lights burning. With a sudden whoosh, the object hovered above us, maybe five hundred feet in the air. The white light lit up the area like the noonday sun. We fell trembling to our faces on the truck bed. The light exploded into fiery orange and disappeared!

A holy awe gripped us, and we found ourselves suspended in the glory. Even the crickets hushed their song. I thought of the verse, *He makes His angels ministering flames of fire*. On the night Jesus was born, angels appeared to shepherds in the field and the glory lit up the sky. Now I understood why the angels said, "Fear not."

The next night we told the Bible study group how God answered Mark's simple prayer with an awesome visitation. The students shouted and celebrated, and great expectancy gripped the believers on campus.

One day a woman said to me, "You're from Tulsa, you must know about Kenneth Hagin."

"Who's Kenneth Hagin?" I said. At that time, all I'd heard about Christians in Tulsa were the negative things my synagogue and family had told me about Oral Roberts. She just smiled and gave me Hagin's book, "What Faith Is."

I read the book, and during semester break I attended Brother Hagin's healing class at Rhema Bible Training Center. He spoke under a powerful anointing, telling us of his boyhood days when the glory cloud rolled into their Pentecostal meetings. "I know about this," I said. "He's talking about what I've seen!"

Hungry to learn more, I immediately withdrew from Missouri Southern and enrolled at Rhema Bible Training Center. For a year I pressed in to learn Scripture and more about the glory realm. Then God directed me to leave Rhema and enter Oral Roberts University. I was to study Hebrew because He was sending me back to the Jewish people.

"Oh, Lord," I pleaded, "send me anywhere, send me to India for the rest of my life. But not to the stiff-necked Jewish people!"

"*No*," He said, "*you need to study Hebrew.*" I bowed my heart to His will. Since I was supporting myself, I worked eagerly that year, saving enough money to attend the University.

Where's the Beef?

I received an excellent education at ORU, but I gradually lost that sweet intimacy with the Lord. I was so busy learning about God that I neglected spending time on my knees searching for the Secret Place with Him. I drifted further and further away, caught up in study and work. His close friendship was no longer over my tent even though I witnessed for him consistently.

I joined an outreach group, The Soul Patrol, that went out on what we called "tract attacks." Sometimes we gathered outside Tulsa's raunchiest bars and witnessed for Jesus until four in the morning. At other times we met in the parking lots outside rock concerts. While heavy metal screeched in the dope-scented air, we confronted the kids with the love of Jesus. God often confirmed our message, supernaturally setting people free and filling them with new life.

The Soul Patrol members shared a radical commitment to obey the Lord. Because we turned our backs on the compromises that divided the hearts of so many students, we saw God's power defeat the power of Satan, week after week. The intensity of those times knitted our hearts so deeply that we would have died for one another. That fervency helped keep my heart's flame burning during the long seasons of academia.

Graduating Summa Cum Laude from ORU in 1987, I received an academic scholarship to continue studying Hebrew and Biblical literature on the graduate level at ORU's Theological Seminary. If my undergraduate days were difficult, my year as a graduate student nearly broke my health and spiritual vitality. Mistakenly believing that academic achievement would somehow turn my parents to the faith, I drove myself to maintain a perfect 4.0 grade point average on a full load of eighteen credit hours. My scholarship required me to proctor, teach and grade one hundred and fifty undergraduate students while I slogged through my thesis in Ugaritic studies on the subject of the afterlife in the post-exilic literature of ancient Israel.

Those days began at 3 a.m. when I got up to deliver bundles of newspapers to convenience stores until seven in the morning. By May, this grind had worn me to the ragged edge.

Early one afternoon at the close of the spring semester, two guys came into my room. "Scott, put down the pencil. You're too wrapped up in the school-work, man. Let's go pray." We walked out of the graduate housing complex and over to the banks of the Arkansas River, a tributary of the Mississippi. A hydroelectric dam twenty miles upstream leaves the river flowing shallow through Tulsa. And the unusually dry spring had lowered the waters even more. We began to worship the Lord, and my heart felt as dry as that parched riverbed.

I looked at the two guys with me. One, a German, was standing there proclaiming God's purposes over entire continents. The other, an Arab, was praying for God to send him to the Shiite Moslems for martyrdom. And here I stood a Jewish kid from Oklahoma, weary of studying past revivals and seeing so little of the real thing and felt like we were the three stooges. A sudden hunger for the living God gripped me. I jumped onto a picnic table and cried out with all my might.

"Where's the God of Elijah? Where's the beef?" I didn't speak out of disrespect to the Lord. I was just suddenly desperate for God to show me His glory again. Then a mantle of prophecy dropped on me, and the Lord spoke.

"Son, prophesy to this dry river, for by this time tomorrow, the Arkansas River will be at flood stage as a sign to you

41

of the power, the glory and the finances coming into the Church in the last days." Carried along by this anointing, I prophesied for nearly thirty minutes. When the mantle lifted, we walked away. "I know that was the Holy Ghost," I told my friends. "But I've lived in Tulsa all my life. It's going to take an awful lot of rain to flood that river. How's God going to do it?"

I went back to my room. When I returned to writing my thesis, the familiar chain snapped again around my neck and the walls closed in. Someone burst into the room. "Come here, man! Jim Bakker...the PTL Club! A huge scandal just broke!"

We crowded around a TV, joining the largest audience *Nightline* ever had. Tammy Bakker cried while Ted Koppel questioned Jim Bakker who kept trying to repent before America. Mocking voices in the TV room yelled at Jim Bakker's remorseful image, demanding he answer Koppel's questions. The mantle of prophecy fell on me again. I heard the Lord's still, sweet voice say, *"I'm going to restore Jim Bakker to ministry because of his repentant heart."* At that moment, thunder cracked, the clouds burst and torrents of rain beat down on the roof! The next morning, University officials ordered us to evacuate the graduate housing complex. We grabbed a few things and drove out as volunteers were now marching in to build sandbag barriers. The Arkansas River now flooded past the picnic table where I stood prophesying the night before. A mammoth storm had parked over Tulsa, dumping four to eight inches of rain on different areas of the city. The media called it the "Great Tulsa Flood of 1987." The Lord spoke, the heavens opened and the river flooded. The dramatic, next-day fulfillment of the prophetic word over the Arkansas River electrified me and my friends. We believed the great revival would break out that week. But God's real showers of blessing were not to begin for another two years.

After completing my first year of graduate studies at Oral Roberts University, I spoke by phone with Dr. Michael L. Brown. He invited me to come to Gaithersburg, Maryland and study at the Messianic Yeshiva that he headed under Beth Messiah Congregation. I packed up and drove cross-country to the northern suburbs of Washington D.C. Two weeks later I met Dalit Gorelik at Beth Messiah. During the following months our relationship deepened. When I asked Dalit to marry me, she

 said yes. When we told the leadership, one of their wives said she'd just had a prophetic dream of who I was to marry. Dalit was not the one. I sensed the still small voice confirming Dalit was the one sent to stand at my side, bear our children and fulfill her part in whatever ministry the Lord had for us. We obeyed His voice rather than the voices around us,

Our Wedding Day June 18, 1988

and the Lord's presence came in power during our wedding. Sadly, the other woman seen in the dream later drifted back into the world. I count myself blessed of the Lord for sending Dalit to me.

> **O my dove, in the clefts of the rock, in the secret place of the steep pathway, let me see your form, let me hear your voice; for your voice is sweet, and your form is lovely.**
>
> **Song of Solomon 2:14**

43

Dalit's past and heritage bring unique dimensions to our family and ministry. Her parents became believers in Communist Russia during Stalin's reign. Her Jewish father was a gifted artist, training at the Art Institute of Leningrad, when he became a believer at age fifteen.

His parents thought he'd lost his mind when he began speaking in tongues and left the famous art institute. In true Russian Soviet tradition, they committed him to a mental hospital. For three months the doctors evaluated and tested him but found nothing wrong with him.

Dalit with her parents on our wedding day

Dalit's grandmother was imprisoned for selling meat on the black market during World War II. At age twelve, Dalit's mother and her brothers were left to fend for themselves until their mother's release. During those dark days, Dalit's mother was born again.

The eldest of seven children, Dalit grew up in the Russian underground church. In 1973, when she was ten years old, a door strangely opened and the family immigrated to Israel.

A month after they reached the land, the Arab nations attacked on Israel's holiest day of the year, Yom Kippur. Syrian shells exploded only six kilometers from their apartment in the immigrant community of Nazareth Elit. Dalit remembers a day when the artillery shells sent their neighbors running to the bomb shelter, while her family stayed home. Her mother had prayed and the Holy Spirit told her nothing would harm them.

There was scant spiritual nourishment or fellowship during those difficult days in Israel and much persecution and ridicule at school for young believers in Yeshua, Jesus. Dalit's walk with the Lord further deteriorated during her teen-age years.

Her father had a prophetic dream to move to America, and within two weeks they had sold everything. However, Dalit remained in Israel, choosing to serve in the IDF, the Israel Defense Forces.

She was assigned as a clerical secretary to a ranking officer in the elite Commando unit, "Golani." Dalit took her stand for Yeshua, knowing she'd continue to suffer ridicule and estrangement for her faith. They soon demoted her to a social worker's position, giving her the task of notifying the families of soldiers killed in action. She set her heart on becoming a Drill Sergeant for the Golani Brigade, but her desire was met with mocking and laughter.

One day, awaiting her new orders, Dalit wept. Someone suggested that she go to a nearby kibbutz where Chief of Staff Raphel Etan lived. Etan held the highest rank in the Israeli army, and was the only high level officer who opened his heart like a father to the soldiers. A few days later Dalit knocked on his door. "Come in," he said. "Sit down, have some coffee. Now tell me what's your problem?"

She poured out her heart to the top man in the IDF, telling him her trials and frustrations as a female soldier who believed in Jesus.

"So what would you like me to do for you?" he said.

"I want to be a Drill Sergeant in the Golani, or I am going to leave the IDF," Dalit said. Now that's "chutzpah."

Raphel Etan kindly sent her on her way. Days later, eyes opened and mouths closed when orders came down from the top, promoting Dalit to Drill Sergeant in the Golani Brigade!

She worked hard, drilling the recruits through the torturous obstacle course. Her tour of duty came during the

1982 war in Lebanon, and many of those young men were killed in action. That was a trying time for her unit and for the whole nation. But God was building backbone and courage into this young woman, knowing the calling He had prepared for her.

Dalit's tenure of duty with the Golani Brigade

When Dalit's tour of duty ended she studied physical education and earned a teaching certificate in Israeli folk dancing from the Wingate Institute of Israel. Later, she came to the United States and visited her family. Disheartened by her impressions of American believers, she planned on returning to Israel.

"Beth Messiah Congregation was only a stopping off place before I returned to Israel," Dalit said. "But there I met Scott and I fell in love with him. His zeal for the things of God helped revive me from my backslidden condition. He made me hungry to have the joy and liberty he enjoyed with God. I could feel the heaviness and pain of my past fading when I saw the freedom and healing that a deeper relationship with Jesus could bring."

Dalit and I were married June 18, 1988. Our goal was to move to Israel as soon as possible. I went to work in the mailroom of Sid Roth's Messianic Vision ministry, and we tried settling into a comfortable suburban life. One day at the end of November, 1991, a missionary named Vicki Fugent came to our staff prayer meeting. Moved by the Spirit, Vicki prophesied Isaiah 43:18-21 over the staff.

"Do not call to mind the former things, or ponder the things of the past.

"Behold, I will do something new, now it will spring forth; will you not be aware of it? I will even make a roadway in the wilderness, rivers in the desert.

"...To give drink to My chosen people.

"The people whom I formed for Myself, will declare My praise."

I pondered those verses over and over, feeling something new stirring in my spirit. A long time had passed since I'd thought of the Arkansas River flood. Not only was Jim Bakker not restored but he was serving a fifty-year prison sentence. "The only ministry Bakker will ever have," said one Beth Messiah elder mockingly, "is a prison ministry!"

A week later, Richard Cannon walked into the mailroom, and we talked together.

"Listen," I said, "the Holy Spirit is stirring Dalit and me to leave Maryland. We're moving up to Brooklyn to reach the Jewish people." Suddenly Richard broke into joyous weeping and he prophesied over me saying, *"My word that you'll bring forth, says the Lord, will be like Rivers in the Desert, bringing the refreshing to My people."* There was that exact same portion of scripture from the Eighth Century Old Testament prophet Isaiah again! What was God saying to us?

When I went to work the following day, my heart pounded as I recalled how God confirmed the prophetic word with the Arkansas River flash flood of 1987. I tried speaking at our ministry prayer meeting, but somehow I couldn't communicate to the others my growing conviction that God was about to do something new. The day after that, December 5, 1991, I switched on the mailroom radio and heard a news bulletin. "Today Israel is experiencing major flash flooding in the desert regions of the Negev...." I was stunned and suddenly understood what God was saying! Something powerfully new was now happening on planet Earth!

In the days that followed, I quickly collected articles from the Jerusalem Post. The December 14, 1991 edition reported that severe winter storms from the previous week had generated country wide rainfall which far exceeded the average monthly total for November and reached an intensity not matched in half a century. The paper said that the storms caused major traffic disruptions, severe damage to crops and various installations, widespread flooding in cities and along the coast. They said that the coastal town of Ashdod was the worst hit and that even in the Negev desert and Gaza, record amounts of rain amassed and in some places stopped traffic, requiring emergency crews, police and IDF units to carry out rescue evacuations. They reminded us that only once previously in this century, in December 1941, were comparable rains registered.[1]

I read that the record-breaking winter continued with no end to the wet, stormy weather in sight; that heavy snow was reported on the northern reaches of the Golan Heights, closing roads in the region, and snow was even expected in the Negev. They reported a flood alert had been declared on the Golan Heights, in areas bordering the northern reaches of the Jordan River and the already flooded Hula Valley; and that the main concern on the Golan centers was the stability of four already full reservoirs. The newspaper reported that the dam, near Kibbutz Degania Alef, was expected to be opened before the water level neared the maximal mark, to prevent the lake filling too quickly and flooding parts of Tiberias, as well as settlements on the shore of Kinneret.[2]

The rain that deluged the nation of Israel that winter turned into the worst weather recorded in living memory and surpassed all rainfall totals since records were first kept in 1904; and was later coined as "the winter the skies fell in!" for this tiny arid country.[3]

Listen attentively to what God is saying in all this meteorological activity, dear friends! In Isaiah 43:18-21, this eighth century prophet admonished the people of God in his generation to look for a momentous transition about to take place. He exhorted them to stop pondering the former things, to forget the successes and failures of their past. They had to remove all the old leaven of experiential knowledge so that they could become a new lump. Isaiah was pent-up with a holy passion for Israel to awaken and heed what was about to happen in their midst.

To confirm Isaiah's words, God promised to give the people a natural sign of such staggering dimensions that it would seize their attention and catapult them off their blessed assurance. This natural sign would be *naharot byishimon*, raging floods and rivers in the desolate regions of the Dead Sea, the Negev and the Arabah. Not just a localized flash flooding of some dry wadi bed, but an unrivaled deluge of rain that would cause even the desert wasteland to blossom.

This event would be a sign to the people of God in Isaiah's time (and to the generations in the future) that a transition was commencing in the economy of God.

Isaiah continued speaking of an outpouring of the Holy Spirit in chapter 44:3:

"For I will pour out water on the thirsty land and streams on the dry ground; I will pour out My Spirit on your offspring and My blessing on your descendants."

The reading of this text in the Hebrew reveals some exciting facts. First, the sentence in verse three can also be translated from the prepositions in Hebrew, *Even as I will pour water on the thirsty lands, so will be the same measure I will pour out My Spirit on your offspring.* Praise God, this means that when record setting rains deluge the desert areas of Israel, get ready for a corresponding measure (and even greater) of the Holy Spirit to fall in a new way worldwide!

Second, in verse one Isaiah uses the most popular phrase in all of Judaism, *Shema Yisrael*, or "Hear O Israel," to galvanize the people's attention to this event. The word for hear used above stems from the same word for a hearing heart, *shema*.[4] He used this phrase to startle the people out of their familiarity with its daily use in the temple liturgy, and shake them into understanding that God would soon do something unprecedented in their midst.

We may not be able today to verify through archeology that a massive rainfall occurred in Israel during the winter preceding the day of Pentecost, but we do know for certain that massive rains deluged the land of Israel during the winter of 1991-92.

I have amazing photos of the Gaza Strip looking like Bangladesh after a monsoon. Other pictures show Jerusalem under twenty inches of snow. Massive flooding flashed through desert lands around Jerusalem. Newspaper articles described excited botanists with species of flowers suddenly blooming in the desert after lying dormant for centuries. Growing up in Israel, Dalit had never seen anything like this before.

The biblical pattern of the eighth century prophets of the Old Testament was to use natural conditions to describe the activity of the Kingdom of God. One example of this is the way that natural events occurring in the land of Israel can herald what God is about to do in the Church. Though unknown at the time, something significant was poured into the Body of Christ in North America during those floods in the Israeli desert. During that winter, the Holy Spirit began flowing in power through the ministry of a young missionary from South Africa, Rodney Howard-Browne. This yielded servant of God was one of the point men for the revival now beginning to spread throughout this continent. Many churches of diverse affiliations have since become oases of refreshing and revival for millions of thirsty visitors worldwide.

> **Restore our captivity, O Lord, as the streams in the South** [Negev].
>
> **Psalms 126:4**

As I write this in May of 1999, I believe God is continuing to bring about a significant transition to the Body of Christ worldwide. He is reviving our first love and renewing us to serve Him with joyful and passionate vigor. Soon we'll see the next wave of glory confirming the Gospel with increasingly powerful signs, wonders and miracles to bring in the harvest of lost souls. This will be called the Third Great Awakening, and it is knocking at our door even now!!! Surfers catch the big waves by first seeing them coming, then positioning themselves and paddling up to speed. Otherwise, the wave surges past beneath them or crashes upon them. Don't miss this next wave now forming on the horizon. There's never been anything like it before.

Stepping Out

In 1990, Sid Roth founded the congregation "Mayim Chayyim," which is Hebrew for "Living Waters," in Brooklyn, New York. While I continued working in the mailroom, Dalit and I joined others in outreach thrusts into the Jewish community in New York City, sponsored by that fledgling congregation. There we got our first taste of bringing the Gospel both to hardened New York Jews and especially to the tens of thousands of Russian Jews flooding into that area.

Russian Jewish immigrants hearing the Gospel message during outreach event at Mayim Chayyim Congregation

In 1992 Dalit and I relocated our family of four to Brooklyn to serve as associate pastors of Mayim Chayyim, under Sid Roth's oversight. We left our prosperous suburban neighborhood in the rolling farmland of Maryland, and bunji jumped into the shabby, brutal life of Brooklyn's Russian immigrant community. Police and ambulance sirens blared at all hours, a psychic lived downstairs from our small apartment and gunfire felled a man in front of our building. But our ministry bore fruit; and that spurred us on.

Welcome to Brighton Beach — home for over 100,000 Russian Jews

Moscow or New York?

Brooklyn's Russian immigrant community

The congregation first met in a Brooklyn nightclub. Hundreds of Russian Jews made decisions for Yeshua, but only 70 converts came to our discipleship class. Because of her fluency in Russian, Dalit did much of the interpreting. This naturally resulted in many of the Russians dumping their horrific problems on her. After grueling months of fulfilling her role as wife and young mother to Gideon and Deborah, the ministry became nearly overwhelming for Dalit.

The Russians who truly knew the Lord continued on with God, and we were deeply thankful for them. However, many who raised their hands for salvation never submitted to His commandments. Some Russians came to us only to get refugee status as Jews under religious persecution for supposedly believing in Jesus. Deception is an integral part of Russian society, and that didn't change while these immigrants struggled to build a new life in the hard places of Brooklyn.

Meanwhile, Sid Roth relocated the Messianic Vision ministry to Georgia and flew up to Brooklyn once a month to oversee Mayim Chayyim. This proved a difficult arrangement for all of us. We begged various churches to lend a hand, but no real help came. When tensions reached what we thought were their worst point, the Ultra-Orthodox Jews showed up.

Week after week, like a constant dripping, they protested outside our meetings. Some exchanged their black suits and hats for regular street clothes and entered our services masquerading as seekers. They'd lean over and whisper to the Russians, "If you come here we'll have your social security cut off." Their rabbis teach a concept they call "the heavenly lie," claiming it's a righteous thing to lie if it saves a Jewish soul from Christianity. All too familiar with the intimidating tactics of the KGB back home, the Russians often believed these lies and fled from our services.

Police guard against escalating aggression from the Ultra-Orthodox Jews

Orthodox Jewish demonstrator against our services

Then the Ultra-Orthodox sabotaged our car, our meetings and our outreach events. Their escalating aggression required twelve to fifteen New York City police officers taking up regular positions outside the doors of our building. To enter our church, you had to clutch your Bible and run like a fullback through the jeering crowd of blaspheming protesters until you reached the barricades at the doors.

The police did nothing to really protect our Constitutional rights beyond maintaining a passive presence. That was an election year, and the mayor didn't want to jeopardize the powerful Jewish vote. The precinct Chief came on Saturday mornings and stood around. We were a flash point in the neighborhood, and the City Administration made it clear to the Ultra-Orthodox that they did not favor our church.

Police protection by NYCPD in front of our weekly services

On top of all these difficulties, most of our congregation never matured, so we constantly dealt with baby believers. "Lord," I prayed, "why don't our people mature in the Holy Spirit?" I heard Him reply, *"The occult."*

So I preached on the occult, and during the altar call I asked the congregation, "Who here has been involved with the occult?"

"None of us," they said, "we're not involved in the occult. What's the occult?"

"Let's make this easier," I said. "Who's been involved in Tarot cards, or ESP?"

"Oh yes, ESP," said one. "I have a doctorate in ESP!"

"I'm known as an ESP healer," said another.

I learned then that the Russians are world leaders in this whole field, with occultic powers even harnessed for the military. Many of our congregation were occultists, well trained in seeing auras, sticking needles in parts of people's bodies, and a host of other demonic practices.

Needless to say, we had a lot of discipleship to do following that morning service, and the realization of true Soviet culture.

After our translator left I discovered that a woman on the music team was moving in control, directing the lives of as many people as she could. Throughout all this, Dalit and I had no real fellowship to refresh us. We came under financial pressure and our marriage and home life suffered severe strain.

We moved the congregation into an old movie theater, and began showing the "Jesus" movie. The Ultra-Orthodox were incensed that Russian Jews came to this outreach and made decisions for Christ. In protest, they screamed to drown out the PA system that played the sound track on the sidewalk.

Though Dalit had reached the point of burnout, she nevertheless refused to back down. One Saturday, she stood on the sidewalk debating with three rabbis in Hebrew. Suddenly one of these men grabbed her arm, swung her around and tried to throw her in front of a

Dalit witnessing to Jewish protesters on the sidewalk

passing car. I was preaching inside when I heard that, and anger blazed inside me

I was about to dash over to the glass cabinet housing an emergency fire hose, powerful enough to drench the entire theater. I wanted to drag the long hose upstairs to the nursery window and blast them on the sidewalk below. Instead of that senseless act, I stopped the service and we prayed for the Ultra-Orthodox, asking God to turn those Sauls into Pauls.

I called for the congregation to pray forgiveness over those Jewish rebels. Only later did I understand how this forgiveness was a turning point in our ministry. However, I decided that I could no longer leave my family in this crisis situation. Desperate for more of God's life, we stood at a crossroads in our lives and ministry. At that critical hour, someone showed us a ministry video from Rodney Howard-Browne.

The River Begins

"Is this really God?" Dalit said.

"Yeah," I said, "I don't understand everything he's saying. But I sense the same thing I experienced in the Missouri college revival in 1979."

Breathing in the sweetness of the wind of the Spirit, I just had to have more. We left Gideon and Deborah with Dalit's sister, and drove off to Louisville, Kentucky for two weeks. We found our way to the 1993 Campmeeting, and after two days of extraordinary meetings, the power of God gripped Dalit. Brother Rodney called us forward and prophesied, saying, "The Jews in New York City need signs and wonders."

During the difficult months that followed, we clung to our faith believing we would see that word fulfilled. That hope spurred us on to seek diligently for the Lord in the Secret Place.

Chapter 3
Tornado Vision

Behold, the tempest of the Lord! Wrath has gone forth, a sweeping tempest; it will burst on the head of the wicked.

The fierce anger of the Lord will not turn back until He has performed and until He has accomplished the intent of His heart; in the latter days you will understand this.

Jeremiah 30:23,24

When I was a teenager and an unbeliever, I dreamt I saw a black tornado roaring towards our home. In my dream I knew that if I didn't repent and obey the call to preach, the swirling fury would destroy our home and hurl me into outer darkness. I awoke, seized with the fear of God.

The River Comes to Brooklyn

Report of the Schneerson event reached Rodney Howard-Browne during his meetings on Long Island. He met with Sid Roth and me, and agreed to minister at our church. We were amazed that he would come from overflow meetings of thousands to our congregation of only 120 people. And when he came, most of the religious Russians left.

The Spirit moved in power during that service bringing conviction, but many refused to repent. When

59

they rejected God's offer of power and freedom, Dalit and I realized that we, too, would soon leave Mayim Chayyim.

The River Hits Brooklyn, NY — Mayim Chayyim Congregation

Those of us who had welcomed the river enjoyed meetings lasting five, six and seven hours. We soaked in God's manifest presence and worshiped our Savior with overflowing hearts.

While Tom Nicholson preached one of these services, our five year-old firstborn, Gideon, toppled off his seat onto the floor. He rolled back and forth seized with holy laughter, except that he made no sound. Nothing. He laughed and laughed, but silently!

After an hour of this, I stirred Gideon out of his joy and demanded that he explain.

"Abba," he said, "Jesus is tickling me!"

"Oh no," I thought to myself, "God's visiting my son and I'm fearful and trying to pull him out of it."

I felt no bigger than a toadstool, but Gideon didn't stop. He rolled on the floor, laughing and throwing his sweater and shoes. Dalit laughed so hard that she nearly went into labor with our third child. Just then I sensed the awesome presence of the Lord Jesus, standing behind my left shoulder.

"The Lord's in this place," Tom said. "I feel like repenting!" Tom suddenly stopped preaching and then stepped back from the center aisle, as if making way for Jesus, though he didn't see Him. When the Lord walked past me, His presence electrified my whole being. It was as if the lens of my mind closed, and the eye of my spirit opened. I knew He was not an angel, but the Lord Himself. When I opened my eyes, I saw the back of the Lord's head and torso disappear through the wall. He spoke to me, and His words drew me after Him.

"Follow Me, and I'll make you a fisher of men."

That day I decided to leave the pastorate, turn the congregation over to another couple, and go out preaching from church to church. We were grateful to Sid Roth for giving us our first position in full-time ministry, but the time had come for moving on.

A Gift

The Brooklyn congregation gave us a farewell party, and presented me with a gift — a shofar. This shofar was not the small ram's horn, but the larger Yemenite shofar from the antelope called the Kudu. This trumpet has the rugged character of locusts and wild honey, of camel's hair and leather.

It's made by hollowing out the horn of this huge African antelope. When new, these shofars stink of the flesh of the antelope until soaked in bleach. Sometimes I feel like a new shofar in the hands of the Master, being emptied and stretched, the heat of His dealings burning up my flesh, making me a useful channel for His purposes.

Back then I thought it was absolutely ridiculous to carry around a shofar and blow it. I thanked our friends for the gift, planning to stick it on a bookshelf as a momento of our years in Brooklyn. The people insisted I blow the thing but I refused. I had once tried sounding Tom Nicholson's shofar and nearly gave myself a hernia!

I handed the shofar to a professional trumpet player, but she couldn't make a clear sound. She handed it back. I felt the anointing come on me. My fingers settled between the horn's bony ridges. Breath rushed out of me. TRUHaaAHH! I was amazed to hear that powerful sound, and I've had the shofar with me ever since.

Of course the power is not in this antelope horn. The power flows through obeying God's still small voice. No one can choose to blow a shofar and presume that God's signs and wonders will follow. Nor do I imagine I'm the only one called to prophetically blow the shofar under God's anointing.

Scott blowing the Yemenite shofar, made from the antelope called the Kudu for their fifth baby dedication

Stepping Out

After the birth of our second daughter, Yael, the five of us moved to another place in Brooklyn. On February 15, 1995, the Lord sent us out again on a shofar exploit. Dalit and I drove into New York City where we met Tom Nicholson and some other friends.

We drove into midtown Manhattan as the day surrendered to the dazzling lights of Times Square. We pulled over and got out in front of a large and influential church. This congregation's founder and leader has been mightily used of God, preaching the Gospel in the midst of Broadway's glittering cesspool. But God told me to blow the shofar and shake the place as a prophetic sign in the Spirit. This was a warning to the pastor for his continued public criticism of the Toronto Blessing and Rodney Howard-Browne's ministry. I blew the shofar, and we headed down to Wall Street.

We've since learned that the next day, February 16, several key leaders and staff left the church.

It was dark when we reached the southern end of Manhattan. We turned onto Wall Street, parked and stood before the massive stone edifice housing the New York Stock Exchange. Icy winds blew in off the water and stung our faces as we raised our shofars. We blew long, piercing blasts of judgment. The front doors of the Stock Exchange flew open, and security guards rushed us.

"Quiet," they yelled. "They're shooting a big Hollywood movie in there. You're ruining the sound track!"

But Tom and I blew one blast after another until we felt a release to stop. A police car pulled up and two young officers got out.

"What's with all the noise?" said one officer.

"God told us to come here to pray," we said.

"Thank God," he said. Amazed at his reply, we asked this believer what was going on.

"This weekend is the anniversary of the World Trade Center bombing," he said. "We've had a major bomb threat here on Wall Street. When we heard that sound we thought a bomb was about to blow!"

One of our group ministered to the other officer and he prayed to receive Jesus. "I'm so thankful," said the first officer as they left. "I know we'll be OK tonight."

"Lord," I said, "what's this mean here tonight?"

Then in my spirit I saw the Dow Jones rise higher and higher until it went through the roof. Then it was to later suddenly plunge down. Eight days later, the Dow Jones soared past 4000 for the first time in history.[1] We've seen the bull market rise past 11,000 since blowing the shofar at the NYCSE that night of February 15, 1995, and one day we'll also see it crash.

It's no bull! Dow climbs past 6,000

Dow shatters the 7000 barrier

Dow breaks 8,000

Dow 10,000 at last!

Dow Smashes Through 11,000

*After blowing the shofar at the New York City Stock Exchange,
the market rose radically*

The Rivers in the Desert

The time came to incorporate our ministry, Rivers in the Desert International. My first international trip took me to Canada, to Newfoundland's Cape Spear, the eastern most tip of North America.

During the winter, unrelenting fog and towering slabs of broken iceberg clogging the harbor confine the fishing boats to their berths. I took the pastors to the top of Signal Hill, pointed at the fog bank and blew the shofar. We watched a south wind begin dispelling the mist above us like a hair dryer clearing a widening circle on a fogged mirror.

Newscasts marveled at the phenomenon of clear skies suddenly appearing over the area. Reports quickly spread of how the shofar blast opened the skies, and drew people to the meetings from up to four hours away. The next night, the wind cleared the ice from the whole bay.

One day God gave me a vision. I saw the heavens open and myriad's of warrior angels on chariots of fire stream down through Cape Spear. I described this vision to the pastor with me. "Here's where many of the early ships coming to America first stopped," he said. "This is the gate of North America."

65

Puppets of the Antichrist

After fourteen days of glorious revival meetings, I flew on to Halifax, Nova Scotia. While I sat alone in the plane during the layover, the Lord whispered to my spirit.

"You need to pray right now!"

Gripped with an intense burden, I began interceding in the Spirit. A wicked and powerful presence seeped into the plane and settled around me.

"This is worse than New York City," I said to myself.

"Would you like a newspaper?" said the stewardess.

I took the newspaper to hold open in front of me while I prayed. The headline read, "G7 Economic Summit Begins Next Week." The world's economic leaders were about to meet in Halifax. I turned the page. "Famous Buddhist Monk to Inaugurate First Heaven on Earth Day." The article detailed how more than 100,000 people were converging on Halifax for this occultic celebration.

"These are puppets of the Antichrist, intercessors of darkness," I heard the Spirit say. *"They're preparing the way for the economic summit to plan the one-world currency."*

New Agers from all walks of life filled up the airplane, excited about the apparent success of their convocation. I looked up from the article about the old Buddhist monk to see him come shuffling down the aisle, followed by his entourage. This stooped shell of a man sat down across the aisle from me. His frail fingers began to worry his prayer beads and he sank into deep meditation.

"Pray now," the Lord said.

"Lord God, I call the fire of your love upon this man. Set him free from his demonic captors so he can see Jesus!"

I faced the monk and spoke to the unclean spirits. "I bind you in Jesus Name!" The old monk shook, surfaced from his trance and fastened his demonic glare upon me. I returned to interceding and he sank back into meditation.

Again I felt his uncleanness brush against me. Again I bound the spirits, disturbing the monk's trance. We spent the rest of the flight battling across the aisle, while his followers slept. After we landed in Newark, three lesbians from the group mocked me outside the airport terminal.

I returned home, and rejoiced telling Dalit how the shofar anointing operated everywhere I went. Two months later, we gave up our house, put our things into storage, and with our three children set out on the road to minister from church to church. We had exactly one invitation.

On the Road

Fifteen people jammed the pews for our first meeting at a small church in Delaware. Later that month, the pastor showed us to a rustic, missionary furlough home. Dalit looked around the picturesque house, built before the Civil War.

"It's so romantic," she said. "Let's stay here. It's like Anne of Green Gables."

We threw our bags on the bed and put the kids down for the night. I fumbled for my toothbrush and turned on the tap. The water ran red with rust from the pipes and iron oxide in the old well. We turned off the lights and settled down, only to discover that we were not alone. Mice scampered and gnawed in the walls and rafters. I couldn't sleep.

"Is this how you provide for your wife and kids?" I said to myself. "What kind of father are you? Taking your family from a comfortable house, a steady salary and a congregation you risked your lives to build. For what? This mice-infested house, fifteen people in the meetings and no more invitations?"

Altar

One night, a woman stood up in the meeting and prophesied to us. *"Put your Isaac on the altar and I'll make it a nation."* Immediately it hit me. Our Isaac was the work in Brooklyn. We labored there for several years, withstood the Ultra-Orthodox attacks, found the Secret Place and finally began moving in the revival anointing. Now God showing us that only when we are willing to die to the old does He give a vision for the new. Dalit and I bowed our hearts and placed the Brooklyn work on the altar.

Almost every night for two months, tornadoes had appeared in Dalit's dreams. And now, the very week we put Brooklyn on the altar, God gave me a prophetic dream.

Tornado Vision

In my dream I stand with a pastor on the redwood deck of his suburban home. Under blue skies, sprinklers splash water in lazy arcs over green grass. The laughter of children and the songs of birds carry on the breeze, while barbecuing chicken sizzles on the grill.

Turning I see a squall line suddenly darken the horizon. An enormous black funnel drops from the swirling clouds only a few hundred meters away. Twister! I throw open the screen door and burst into the living room, yelling.

"Get into the basement. A twister's coming!"

The believers in the house stop chatting and face me with blank looks. They glance out the curtained windows where white clouds dot the blue sky.

"What're you talking about? There's no twister coming!"

"I'm telling you, there's a twister coming. Hurry!"

I'm trembling in shock from the sudden invasion of the tornado roaring down upon us. But the others hear nothing. They shake their heads and glance to one another. The front door opens and some of the wives bustle into the house, laden with shopping bags from the mall.

"What's Scott talking about?" they say. "We were just outside. There's no twister coming. It is a gorgeous day outside and we're going sun-bathing."

Realizing I can't reach these believers, I throw open a door and dash down to the musty basement. Hearing little footsteps clattering on the stairs, I turn and see all the children following me, their faces sober with understanding. Of all those in the house, only the little ones respond to my warning cry.

"In here, quick!" I yell.

We crowd into the damp bathroom that stinks of mildew. While some children cling to the toilet, others pile into the bathtub. I turn to close the door. Across the basement I see the pastor and his wife sitting behind a table, pouring over bibles and commentaries.

"There's no tornado coming," they say. "God's a good God. This isn't scriptural. Scott's proclaiming false prophetic word!"

I wonder why I'm seeing the tornado vision, since I'm no different than the other believers in the pastor's house. I close the bathroom door with the deafening tornado upon us. Ready to drape myself over the little ones, I cry out in desperate intercession. Just then, the roaring fades and the bathroom becomes the entry portal into the Secret Place of the Most High. His supernatural quietness lifts us beyond time, enveloping us in peace, and safety under the shadow of the Almighty.

When we leave that place we hear the twister overhead. It leaps over the house, then tears away vegetation and uproots trees. Knowing that we've been spared, I start back up the stairs. A little girl grabs my right arm and I look into her face. She has the eyes of a 50-year-old wise woman, and she speaks with prophetic authority.

"You'll be needing this," she says and hands me the shofar. Feeling the shofar's twisted ridges in my hand, I acknowledge God's purposes for it.

Then I run upstairs and outside onto the deck. A dusty haze shades the air and sky. The pastor and the others gather in stunned silence, all of them under conviction for ignoring the tornado warning.

The bordering woods have been torn away revealing a deep valley below. Beyond that, a city stretches far into the horizon. We watch the black squall line sweep over the inner city where distant streetlights blink on in the advancing darkness.

"Look!" someone cries.

Horrified, we watch a total of eleven eerie tornadoes stab down from the clouds and attack the metropolis. White flashes signal snapping power lines. Houses erupt in funnels of debris and yellow school buses toss like toys above the streets. The howling wind carries the screams of people dying within exploding buildings.

Suddenly my heart fills with deep resolve. Shofar in hand, I run down from the deck toward the city, determined to warn the people. I see an enormous electrical transformer in the pastor's yard, previously hidden by the landscaping.

"What's that?" I wonder.

Then I understand how all the light and power for the people in the valley below comes from this transformer on the pastor's land. I dash over a footbridge joining the suburbs to the city, and find myself amid chaos on the streets of New York City. I meet a drunkard who's leaning against a lamppost.

"You must be saved," I cry. "Jesus loves you. Don't go to hell. The twisters are coming!" The Christians had ignored my warning, but this drunk believes me.

"I know they're coming," he says, "but there's nothing we can do. So let's eat, drink and party, for tonight we all die!"

I turn from him and run deeper into the city, sounding the alarm with all my strength. The city streets unroll before me, becoming the eastern Seaboard of North America. I run south, through New Jersey and Maryland, and down into the Carolinas toward Florida. I look back and see the tornadoes pressing hard behind me.

I pause outside a sprawling Cineplex. Two couples walk toward the movie house, their eyes glazed in apathy.

"Don't go in there," I yell. "The twisters are coming. Jesus loves you. Stop!"

Having no ears to hear the warning, they turn away beneath the swirling sky and stroll inside. In a moment, a twister explodes the movie house.

I run on and on, pulling ahead of the tornadoes and reaching the palm tree coastline of Florida. Multitudes throng toward the twisters, slowing me to a walk. It seemed all of North America had flocked into Florida, the great destination of our culture. The children clamor into the magic kingdom, the young lust for one another on the beaches, the mature seek rest from the rat race and the old shuffle toward dreams of balmy leisure.

Bicyclers and skate boarders wheel among joggers and athletes, all of them intent on beautifying their oiled and tanned bodies. I cry out my warning, and everybody stops.

As if on cue, body builders flex, starlets flaunt their bodies, and others act out dramatic scenes. I realize everyone is auditioning for the Jewish movie producers strolling out from their estates. I turn from this madness and run forward, glancing back as the whirling chaos envelopes them all.

The twisters catch me at Key Largo, but they suddenly jump to either side of the island, becoming towering waterspouts churning the Atlantic Ocean and the Gulf of Mexico. I see intercessors on either side of me, most of them women. While they pray, the waterspouts lift into the sky, doing no damage. Looking back past these faithful intercessors, I see an army. Men are one in three among the ranks, the rest women and children. I'm shocked that so many believers really did heed my warning. I turn to face the north, knowing that I must run again up and down the continent, warning God's people and calling them to rise up.

Interpretation

Filled with awe, I awoke knowing immediately the alarming interpretation. The tornadoes represent a future judgment coming upon North America. They are also a warning from God to me that I must obey Him and run as never before, trumpeting the message of revival to North America. I understood that I will be held responsible for many lost souls if I don't run quickly.

A storm of judgment is coming, but we also will receive a storm of His glory (see Isaiah 60:1-3). Now is

the time to stand in the gap and cry out for this unprecedented awakening that is approaching!

The scene at the pastor's house represents the
church in North America, enjoying a level of peace and
prosperity that no other generation has ever experienced
before in church history. The sudden approach of the
deadly twister on such a tranquil day represents the
swiftness of the shaking about to spring like a trap
upon those who are at ease and stagnant in their spirit
(see Zephaniah 1:12).

The wives returning from shopping represent the
time-consuming lusts of the eyes and flesh and the pride
of life which captivate the hearts of so many believers,
snaring them in the vanities of this age. This prompts
a fierce jealousy in God's heart for His people who are
adulterous in their friendship with the world (see
James 4:4,5).

The apathy and unbelief of the believers toward my
warning represents the attitude of many Christians
toward the new thing God is about to do. I received the
revelation of the impending tornadoes only because of
God's grace, for I was no different than the other believers in the house prior to this dream.

The pastor and his wife studying at the kitchen
table in the basement are sodden with teaching, unable
or unwilling to take action. They represent the excess of
teachings in the North American Church. Overfed on
teachings and underfed on how to flow with the Holy
Spirit, many can't stir themselves to decisive action, and
become reactionary against this new move of God.

The children represent those who, regardless of
their age or gender, are heeding the prophetic oracles of
God and humbling themselves in this critical hour. The
bathroom represents the safest place to be during the

coming shaking, the place of utter humility, the camouflaged entrance to the Secret Place of the Most High (see chapter one for further information on how I discovered this place).

Heart-rending intercession from the secret place is the only thing that can avert the retribution coming upon those that are "sitting on their lees," at ease in Zion.

God gave this tornado vision to show His people that we must learn to enter the Secret Place for protection and for understanding. I also understood more clearly how the tranquillity in the bathroom was the essence of abiding in Him. Safe under His mighty wings, we occupied the position of intercession for the others in the pastor's house.

Miami tornado on whirlwind tour

Twister dropping in downtown Miami suddenly on Monday May 12, 1997 following our "Tornado Vision" revival meetings in the Miami area

The huge electrical transformer in the pastor's backyard represents the authority and power God has given the Church to deliver the lost people in the valley (see Matthew 18:18 and Luke 10:18,19). Only after the tornado could we see the transformer, previously hidden behind trees. This uncovering speaks of the power of God, previously reduced to a doctrinal concept, now being restored to the Church as a living reality to be put into action for the people below in the valley of darkness and indecision.

The footbridge shows the Church no longer ignoring the plight of the inner city. We are their only source for light and power. My crossing that bridge represents how our ministry began in New York City.

The masses in Florida illustrate our nation's lust for self-gratification and our fixation on entertainment. The baby boomers and their offspring look to athletes, movie stars and rock bands for role models instead of spiritual leaders, war heroes or statesmen. Rejecting Judeo-Christian values, they've brought a terrible reaping to America.

The armies of God are those heeding the blast of the trumpet in this hour and are preparing themselves as God's Special Forces to liberate the prisoners in the concentration camps of sin and darkness. These obedient believers know their God intimately from the secret place, having a hearing heart attuned to the Spirit's gentle whisper and will correspondingly do unrivaled exploits for His glory in the coming days.

Reap the Whirlwind

Whirlwind is another word for tornado, and we find many places in Scripture where God speaks through this manifestation of His awesome power.

> Then answered the LORD unto Job out of the whirlwind, and said,
>
> Gird up thy loins now like a man: I will demand of thee, and declare thou unto me.
>
> Job 40:6,7 (KJV)

> The Lord is slow to anger and great in power, and the Lord will by no means leave the guilty unpunished. In the whirlwind and storm is His way, and clouds are the dust beneath His feet.
>
> Nahum 1:3

> Then the Lord will appear over them, and His arrow will go forth like lightning; and the Lord God will blow the trumpet [Hebrew – Shofar], and will march in the storm winds of the south.
>
> Zechariah 9:14

> Behold, the whirlwind of the LORD goeth forth with fury, a continuing whirlwind: it shall fall with pain upon the head of the wicked.
>
> The fierce anger of the LORD shall not return, until he have done it, and until he have performed the intents of His heart: in the latter days ye shall consider it.
>
> Jeremiah 30:23,24 (KJV)

Notice that it's during the latter days, the end times, that we shall consider and understand this. [Author's note: On several occasions, we have publicly shared the "Tornado Vision"; and the following day or week tornadoes have dropped in that same region without warning.]

In September of 1998, following the release of Kenneth Starr's report, a Democratic US Senator quoted from Hosea 7 at a press briefing, declaring of President Clinton and his staff, "They've sown the wind, and they're reaping the whirlwind."

We see the majority of the American people defend-
ing the President's immorality and lying, pointing to the
so-called good economy as reason to keep him in office.
But even as we excuse sin and spit in God's face, we hear
the rumblings of a worldwide financial crisis. And amaz-
ingly enough, even during the 1999 winter impeachment
trial of President William Jefferson Clinton, more tornadoes were spotted (161) during that same month of January than any other January on record. Just in one winter
day, 87 twisters were seen in Arkansas, Louisiana and
Tennessee. Forecasters later said they had no explanation
for this sudden rash of tornadoes![2]

Shaking Wall Street

We had recently settled in a rented house in
Delaware, and though it was especially difficult for
Dalit, in obedience to God's message in the tornado
vision we packed our belongings back into storage and
set out on the road. The first place the Lord sent us was
back up to New York City to blow the shofar on Wall
Street again.

"What's this mean?" I asked the Lord. After our
first time here, the Dow Jones began its unprecedented
climb just as He said. This time there were two significant events for the shofar blowing to release.

"You're signaling a changing of the guard in my body,"
the Lord said quietly from the secret place. *"Like Moses,
the old leaders are dying, and now I'm raising up the Joshua's.
This is also a sign that I'm about to shake the Wall Street
world of business and commerce."*

That night Tom Nicholson joined Dalit and I outside
the Stock Exchange building. Now and then yellow cabs
sped past, but no one walked these deserted streets.
Tom and I blew long, mournful blasts that echoed like
screams in the night among the dark buildings of Wall

Street. No guards rushed out this time. It was just the Lord and us.

Ninety-six hours later, Passover began, recalling the night the death angel killed every first-born in Egypt. Back home in Delaware, Dalit and I watched the moon rise blood red in a full lunar eclipse, the first of the 20th century (see Joel 2:31). That same night a US Air Force jetliner carried Secretary of Commerce Ron Brown and a delegation of American business executives into Croatia. The plane veered off course and crashed into a cloud-covered hill, killing all 33 people aboard![3]

With that tragic part of the Lord's answer confirmed so powerfully in Croatia by the sudden death of the Secretary of Commerce during the night of Passover, I knew God was signaling to us that something big is about to happen in the near future with the Body of Christ obtaining the transference of wealth of the world system like the children of Israel did when they left Egypt. Take some time to ponder this Sixth Century B.C. prophetic oracle meant for our day.

> **"For thus says the Lord of hosts, 'Once more in a little while, I am going to shake the heavens and the earth, and the sea and the dry land.**
>
> **'I will shake all the nations; and they will come with the wealth of all nations, and I will fill this house with glory,' says the Lord of hosts.**
>
> **'The silver is Mine and the gold is Mine,' declares the Lord of hosts.**
>
> **'The latter glory of this house will be greater than the former,' says the Lord of hosts, 'and in this place I will give peace,' declares the Lord of hosts."**
>
> **Haggai 2:6-9**

Later that April, the "Washington for Jesus" organizers invited me to blow the shofar seven times at the close of the rally. During the first night of the event Lester Sumrall went home to Jesus. He personally knew Smith Wigglesworth and represented the final link connecting the old-time Pentecostal revivalists with the young Joshua's of today.

It became clear during the rally that God was positioning His young people in the national spotlight. The

first night only several hundred young people attended the rally, but the following night nearly 500,000 of them thronged the mall. The next day adults were in the minority, joining the record crowd of the Joshua generation as the older ministers laid hands on the new generation of leaders.

Later I took Tom aside. "Let's go down to the White House," I said. "God wants us to blow the shofar there."

Sounding the Shofar during
"Washington for Jesus 1996"

The White House

Tom and I left the rally, drove to a side street, and walked down Pennsylvania Avenue. My spirit burned when I recalled something that had happened in upstate New York, two months before. In February of 1996, I was invited to minister to Reach Out Family Worship Center, at Hyde Park in upstate New York's Hudson River Valley.

"We could hardly get you a room," the church secretary said, "The only motel was nearly full."

I wondered why this small town, site of President Franklin Roosevelt's birth, would be crowded during the frigid New York winter. When I checked in on Saturday night, excitement animated the crowd in the motel lobby.

"What's going on?" I asked the clerk.

"Hillary Clinton is in town," he said. "She and her staff are working across the street in the FDR Library."

I went to sleep, perplexed by a strong presence of spiritual darkness. During the Sunday morning meeting the Holy Spirit interrupted my message, and I began prophesying. "Hillary Clinton and her staff are not researching documents in the FDR Library," I said. "They're holding a séance to contact the spirit of Eleanor Roosevelt!"

The congregation responded, grieved and incensed in their spirits. Late that night, I drove alone to the FDR Mansion. I rolled to a stop in the icy stillness, and sensed the unclean presence of a spirit of sorcery. I blew the shofar, calling for God to expose the true purpose of the First Lady's visit to Hyde Park.

Despite later efforts of White House staffers to squelch the story, the national and international media reported Hillary Clinton's repeated conversations with the departed spirit of Eleanor Roosevelt. Mrs. Clinton spoke openly to sympathetic reporters, saying, "Eleanor usually tells me to buck up, or grow a skin as thick as a rhinoceros."

The White House cleverly explained the séances in New Age terms, passing it off as no more than guided imagery, a motivational exercise. As Elijah burned with anger against Israel's worship of Baal, I now walked toward the White House, infuriated that demonic powers sat enthroned at the highest place in our nation.

Tom and I walked up to the black iron spikes of the fence bordering the front lawn of the White House. When we pulled out our shofars, Secret Service agents leveled telephoto lenses at us from the roof. Other agents sprinted across the lawn, yelling at us.

"What are you guys doing here?"

"We just came to pray," we said. "It's not a protest."

When they realized that we posed no threat they backed away, and watched us blow our shofars over the White House. As always, I asked the Lord for understanding.

"Son," He whispered, *"you're blowing the shofar to expose what's happening in the administration occupying the White House."*

In my spirit I saw the Lord pull on one small insignificant thread of an ornate tapestry, as though unraveling the administration like a knitted garment. When Kenneth Starr later parted the veil of deception shrouding the Clinton White House, we learned a startling fact. Six days after we blew the shofar over the White House, then-deputy White House Chief of Staff Evelyn Lieberman quickly transferred a young intern named Monica Lewinsky to the Pentagon, beginning a small and seemingly insignificant thread of cover-up that was to eventually disgrace and stain the entire administration.[4]

Chapter 4
Jubilee

"**Y**ou shall thus consecrate the fiftieth year and pro-claim a release [liberty] through the land to all its inhabitants. It shall be a jubilee for you, and each of you shall return to his own property, and each of you shall return to his family."

Leviticus 25:10

During the latter half of 1996, I traveled to more and more churches. The power of His anointing increased and we enjoyed God's blessing on our ministry. *"Now,"* said the Lord in the same still small voice He revealed Himself to me two years earlier, *"I want you to blow the shofar for Jubilee for my people."*

I began to search in my Masoretic Hebrew text for the meaning of Jubilee and was so excited to discover that one of the Hebrew words for trumpet is also the same word for the Year of Jubilee, *yobel*.[1] The Year of Jubilee begins with the sounding of the trumpet on Yom Kippur, and this announcement begins the extraordinary favors of God upon His people.

Leviticus chapter 25 outlines the Year of Jubilee as a time when God commanded the land of Israel to rest from cultivation and farming. It was a time that God ordered His supernatural blessings upon the harvest so that the land brought forth great superabundance for several years to come. It was a time that debts were cancelled and

83

slaves were brought back to their own properties and families. In short, it was a time of great rest, joy and prosperity!

Many believers all around the world during the later half of the 1990's began to get excited about the concept of Jubilee for the State of Israel. Mainly due to the fact that the Jewish people, after being decimated by centuries of anti-Semitism, inquisitions, pogroms and the holocaust…were now going to celebrate the 50 years of the establishment of their ancient homeland known today as *Medinat Yisra'el* or the State of Israel. The survival of this tiny country, only slightly larger than the state of New Jersey, after fighting several major wars and being outnumbered on the battlefield and by world opinion, is truly a modern miracle worth celebrating!

As May 1998 approached there was a great prophetic expectancy arising on behalf of many believers of what was to about to happen when the State of Israel officially began celebrating not just Jubilee, but their fiftieth Jubilee or Jubilee of Jubilee's as an ancient people back in their land!

However, in the Word of God I saw a greater plan that we all must see beyond this period of an agricultural festivity and Israel's modern 50 years as a democratic state. The Year of Jubilee is not just a specific linear time frame for God's extraordinary blessings, but we must see clearly that the Year of Jubilee is a person! And His name is Jesus the Messiah!

"The Spirit of the Lord is upon Me, because He anointed Me to preach the gospel to the poor. He has sent Me to proclaim release to the captives, and recovery of sight to the blind, to set free those who are oppressed,

To proclaim *the favorable year of the Lord."*

Luke 4:18,19

The favorable year of the Lord is the Year of Jubilee and its highest fulfillment is not just found in a democratic nation or agricultural festival, but in the anointed One Himself. By examining His ministry we can see that everywhere Jesus traveled He proclaimed the Year of Jubilee or the Gospel (good news) message by forgiving sins, healing the sick, casting out evil spirits, raising the dead, multiplying provisions, and destroying the slavery of religious legalism! This is Jubilee in it's highest fulfillment because it sets the hearts of humanity free from the curse of sin and translates them out from under the pharaoh of this world's system into the adoption as Abba's very own children!

And this Jubilee, that really began 20 centuries ago, will be consummated with the apocalyptic grand finale of the glorious return of Jesus wherein all of creation will be finally set free from the slavery of corruption into the freedom of the glory of the children of God at the resurrection! Glory to God!

Immediately after seeing this in the Scriptures I began proclaiming to the congregations, "God has been leading me to sound the shofar for judgment against false Messiahs and shakings in our government. But now He's also sending me to blow the shofar for the release of Jubilee blessings over the lives of individuals and churches."

For instance, I ministered along these lines at a Tampa church one Friday night. Then suddenly on the following Sunday they received the largest check in the church's history.

"Lord," I said, "this really works!"

I next found myself invited to church after church that all had stepped out in faith for land acquisitions and building projects. I'd blow the shofar for Jubilee and problem loans suddenly came through, zoning laws changed in their favor and cash flow increased. After all the judgments released by sounding the shofar, we rejoiced seeing the Lord also bring these amazing Jubilee blessings. This reminded me of His promise that the Arkansas River flood signaled the coming release of finances into the Church for the last days.

In June of 1996 the Lord directed us to move again, this time from Delaware to Tampa, Florida. I met with Rodney Howard-Browne, already headquartered in Tampa.

"The Lord's telling me to move to Tampa," I said. "What's going on down here?"

"Don't announce anything yet," he said. "I'm starting a church here. God told me it'll be a major refueling hub for ministers based out of Tampa."

"Great," I said, "We're in!"

Preparing to move our family to Tampa, I sounded the Jubilee shofar over a woman's dairy farm in Canada. Her land was embroiled in litigation that threatened their livelihood. We moved to Florida, and found a temporary place in Tampa. Wearied with so much moving, Dalit and I yearned to find a home base for our growing family and ministry.

One day the woman who owned the dairy farm called me. She told how, soon after I blew the shofar, she received an unexpected inheritance of $150,000, and her problems with the dairy farm were beginning to be solved. Not long after that, I opened a letter from her and found a check to us for $10,000!

Determined to build a house, I applied for a building loan, using her gift as a down payment. I was told we didn't meet the bank's criteria of length of employment as a minister with Rivers in the Desert International. All indications pointed to our being turned down. We prayed and I blew the shofar for Jubilee over our circumstance. The loan officer called back.

"I don't understand why," he said, "but it all adds up. Your loan's been approved!"

Hundreds of people gathered at Pastor Rodney's new church, "The River at Tampa Bay," meeting at the Sun Dome. We were refreshed under his teaching, and enjoyed a marked increase of blessing and creativity in our lives. That fall, God stepped up the pace and opened new doors to our ministry. Back in 1994, when I preached at the Toronto Airport Christian Fellowship, I had no idea that a divine connection was being made. Now a phone call opened the way for me into the midst of revival in Montreal.

God's Glory in Montreal

The Canadian National Convention of the Full Gospel Business Men's Fellowship was scheduled to begin in November, 1996. After advertising the services, their keynote speaker fell ill and cancelled. While seeking the Lord for direction, He quickened a passage of Scripture to their hearts from Jeremiah 6:17, "I set watchmen over you, saying, 'Listen to the sound of the trumpet!'..."

In response to that word, the leaders of the convention felt they should find somebody who blew the trumpet. One of them remembered our '94 Toronto Airport meeting, and he called me in Tampa.

"You're supposed to come to our Full Gospel Businessmen's meetings and be our speaker. We don't care what you say, you're supposed to be here!"

"Well pardon me," I thought to myself. "I'm already booked for meetings." But while we spoke, I felt the glory of God fall silently upon me.

"Book me," I said, "I'll be there."

We met in a ballroom at the beautiful Radisson Hotel, in downtown Montreal. During the opening morning meeting in Montreal, I told them about our adventures in Brooklyn, of finding the Secret Place and blowing the shofar outside Lubavitch Headquarters.

That night, the Spirit moved in power and the French Canadians jumped for joy in a spontaneous dance, going wild all around the ballroom. Unbelievers from a business conference in the adjoining hall heard the commotion and ventured into our meeting. The anointing dropped on some of them, and they met Jesus right there.

"I'm blowing the shofar for a mighty tsunami wave," I said. "What we're seeing is just the first drops as God renews us. But we're going to see an awakening!" I later fell off the platform, intoxicated in the new wine of the Spirit.

Heading up to my room that night, I wondered why the elevator car took so long to reach the lobby. The elevator doors parted and I had my answer. Passengers laughed and fell over, filled with the Spirit. After pressing their floor number they'd collapse, dragging their hand down, lighting every button. On the long trip up, the elevator opened at every floor, where I glimpsed people strewn on the carpet, overcome with joy.

I returned home to Tampa, excited by what I felt the Lord would soon do in Montreal. Among French Canadians, less than one percent are born again. I believe God showed me that the French Canadians are the key French-speaking people to reach Central Africa, Haiti and France, which is the only European country that has never seen a nationwide revival.

Amazed to see how God used us as a voice to the Church in Canada, Dalit and I believed this outbreak of the Spirit established an epicenter for a new move of God in this pivotal city of French Canada. And we kept that vision tucked away in our hearts.

Chapter 5
Revival in Canada

R estore our captivity, O Lord, as the streams in the
South [Negev].

Those who sow in tears will reap with joyful
shouting.

Psalms 126:4,5

On January 17, 1997, The Jerusalem Post Daily
Internet Edition reported that rains eases drought.

They proclaimed that the winter drought had been
broken yesterday (January 16, 1997), as rain accompanied by isolated thunderstorms swept most of the
country, causing flooding in many places. They also told
of flash floods closing the road to the Dead Sea and
flooding effecting low areas in the Judean Desert, the
Arava, and the Negev.[1]

In May, while our house was being built, a church
invited me to bring my family and hold ten days of
meetings at St. Hubert, Quebec. I didn't even ask what
kind of church it was. God said go and we went.

In Quebec, I told a reporter for *Arise* magazine,
"Those first meetings were like heaven on earth. The
worship continued for four straight hours." Dalit was
overwhelmed, and felt we had come to receive ministry rather than to minister. The ecstasy she experienced there reminded Dalit of her childhood days in the
underground church in Russia.

For three weeks, the services ran from eight in the evening until as late as six in the morning. Many of the Canadians dripped with sweat, but they didn't care. Having never heard of meetings lasting all night in Canada, one evangelist drove ten hours to be with us, and said he'd never seen anything like it!

There was great joy, but God also gripped many with deep repentance. Some cried out for cleansing from hideous sins, and many backsliders returned to the Father's house. One night, about fifty came to the microphone to confess hidden sins.

"I'm sick of adultery," some men cried out, referring to strongholds of lust in their minds. God broke many, dealing decisively with core issues in their lives. The loving support of humble believers provided a secure setting for confession without fear of being judged.

About 3 a.m. one morning, the Spirit directed that an individual who had left the congregation should be restored. Fifteen people jumped up, got into their cars and drove to the man's house. At 4:30 a.m., they returned, bringing the prodigal with them. It was glorious to see him repent before everyone. Then they set up a receiving line, and for over an hour, the people filed past the man, hugging his neck and welcoming him back home.

The Grand Chief of the Cree Nation, Matthew Coon Come, and his wife attended several of the meetings. God deeply touched their lives, and moved on the French to repent to them for past wrongs against the Canadian Native Indians.

On the Mount

Montreal's foremost landmark is a towering steel cross rising from Mount Royal which overlooks the city. On Friday, July 5, members of the church filled three

Celebration and thanksgiving on Mt. Royal in Montreal, Quebec

school buses and traveled up to Mount Royal. There we
joined five hundred other believers gathered around the
foot of this cross. Many repented for their backslidings,
and we cried out for God to bring an awakening to Montreal. Then I blew the shofar. Shouts of joy and celebration rang out for the next three hours. Many met the
Lord during the altar call, and nearly everybody reded-
icated their lives to Jesus.

Several pastors publicly repented for the sins of the
French against the Jewish people. In response, Jewish pastors stood before the crowd and asked forgiveness on
behalf of the Jewish people who had treated the French
like slave laborers in the past.

God spoke to us from Exodus 34:10 during these
meetings, and it became our theme text.

**Then God said, "Behold, I am going to make a
covenant. Before all your people I will perform miracles which have not been produced in all the earth**

nor among any of the nations; and all the people among whom you live will see the working of the LORD, for it is a fearful thing that I am going to perform with you.

Pharmakeia

The brothers there explained to me how international drug dealers now darkened the face of Montreal and Quebec. They had moved their operations into the Saint Lawrence River Valley, turning stretches of the open border into a major conduit for smuggling narcotics into the United States. That afternoon, God stirred me to prophecy against the international drug trade and then we blew the shofar against the major drug cartel dealers.

U.S. Drug Enforcement Administration officials then later reported that Mexico's most powerful drug lord, Amado Fuentes, died of an apparent heart attack during routine cosmetic surgery, *the next day*. They warned that his death would likely ignite a bloody war for control of the multibillion-dollar Mexican narcotics trade.[2]

During another meeting at the church, the power came upon us and we ran out into the parking lot, yelling and leaping for joy. A man came outside barking at us, "You're all crazy! You're all crazy!" After two weeks of repentance and pure joy, God said He wanted us to take this to the streets.

I told twelve people to go out like twelve spies, drive somewhere and begin witnessing. Several jumped up, gathered others, and left. Three hours later they rushed back in, shouting and dancing. I was telling the congregation how they'd find great joy and see people healed if they began laying their hands on the sick. The "spies" reported that, outside on the streets, they had laid hands on some people and seen them healed and several came to the Lord.

"There's your prophetic sign," I told them. "Twelve spies went out and all twelve returned with a good report. The land is ready. God's about to do something here. We must go to the streets!"

God Divides the Flames

I'd never before felt the dimension of His glory that fell upon us in the streets of Montreal. Virtually everybody we spoke with listened to the Gospel. The Holy Spirit swept over us in waves. Instead of sleeping, we wanted to stay up all night and worship God.

At one point I wept, realizing how Roman Catholicism so strangled the region that when the French Canadians rejected that iron hand of religion they also rejected all spiritual life, leaving a vacuum. Because the young people had no religious experience they were wide open to the true Gospel. Behind the pending referendum

Family time during revival meetings in Montreal, Quebec

whether to separate French and English speaking Canada, is Satan, manipulating the old bitterness and strife. Only a spiritual awakening will truly unify Canada. I see Quebec as a sea of kerosene awaiting revival fires.

After three weeks, the leaders suspended the meetings so the families could spend their summer vacations together. We agreed to return in September and take the meetings to the streets. We drove home with the VCR playing in the van. Our kids were so touched by the revival that all they wanted to watch was a video of the Montreal meetings.

When we stopped at a New Jersey gas station, it was as if the glory rolled out of the van and hit the station attendant. Dalit told him the Lord was coming soon. Conviction hit him, and he gloriously received Jesus right there. Seeing this new anointing for evangelism, we looked forward to the signs and wonders we believed God would soon bring to the streets of Montreal.

Saskatoon

In August, a church in Saskatoon invited me to hold a week of meetings. I flew my family to this vast breadbasket area in Western Canada. God moved again in power, extending one week of meetings into thirteen weeks.

Near the end of our stay, I left my family in Saskatoon and flew to Montreal, eager to see God pick up where we left off that summer. Because of the growing crowds, the meetings were moved to a larger church nearby.

About midnight of the Thursday meeting in Montreal, during Rosh Hashanah, the musicians crossed over into a place called, *"There."* Caught up in the Spirit, the drummer and percussionist played back and forth for ninety minutes. Their pastor later said he'd never experienced the Lord like that during his twenty-five years of ministry. On the platform, intoxicated in the Spirit's overwhelming presence, I suddenly sensed the Lord Jesus standing in front of me.

I opened my eyes but saw no one. I closed my eyes and sensed His silhouette before me radiating light and love. With a clean conscience and no worry clouding my soul, His presence enveloped me. He reached into the very seat of my emotions and peeled back layer after layer, then downloaded pure liquid love into my heart of hearts. This exquisite love turned into excruciating pain when the Lord let me experience the pain He has as He is longingly waiting to come and get His bride.

At 4:30 in the morning, His presence did not lift and I walked out into the crisp Canadian air. Driving back it felt like I was going eighty miles an hour, but the speedometer registered only thirty. I laughed and cried the whole way back to my room. And for three days I remained enfolded in a peaceful haze.

On Sunday night, the week of meetings ended. I packed early, knowing I had to get up at 4:30 in the morning to catch a 6:30 a.m. flight back to Saskatoon. But all through the night I couldn't sleep. I got out of bed, knelt down and prayed until I felt a release. By then it was time to leave for my flight.

Chapter 6
Behold, I Do Something New

"**D**o not call to mind the former things, or ponder things of the past.

"Behold, I will do something new, now it will spring forth; will you not be aware of it? I will even make a roadway in the wilderness, rivers in the desert."

Isaiah 43:18,19

During the week of October 19, 1997, The Jerusalem Post Internet Edition reported that flash floods were ravaging the south. They told of heavy storms over the weekend causing severe flash flooding in the Dead Sea and Negev; and that many of the roads in the Judean Desert and Negev had been completely destroyed in the floods of the last few days; that they were not passable. They reported that the flood damage was totally unprecedented; and that a rare hailstorm in Beersheba had damaged homes and cars and piled up drifts of hailstones to a height of 25 cm.[1]

"Henry," I said, "wake me up when we reach the airport." I settled into Henry Paul's car, the businessman I had stayed with that week in October of 1997. He drove and I slept during the long ride to the airport. Later, his fervent praying in the Spirit woke me. I sensed the spirit of death and knew something was wrong.

"Look," he said, "that car!"

I looked ahead into the *"shahar"* blackness of the pre-dawn. A car on the entrance ramp had jumped the curb and crashed head-on into the end of a guardrail. The twisted car came to a fatal stop under a street-light blocking the entrance ramp of our only way to the airport.

"I can't deal with this now," I said. "I don't even see the driver. Just go around the car."

Weary from fasting and lack of sleep, all I cared about was catching my flight back to my family. Henry cut his Bronco around to the right and drove over the broken glass. We passed beneath the streetlight, and glanced into the car.

"Where's the driver?" I said.

And then we saw her mutilated face, like something out of a horror movie. The shock hit us like a jab to the solar plexus. We nearly vomited. Henry hit the brakes, grabbed his cell phone and called the police. We sat there not wanting to get out, then took a deep breath and opened our doors.

Two truck drivers parked their rigs, and jogged over to the wreck ahead of us. These veteran witnesses of the horrors of highway crashes groaned and turned away, knowing there was nothing they could do. My heart raced as my legs brought me closer and closer to her lifeless body.

The young woman's blonde hair hung outside the passenger window. She'd been thrown from the driver's seat into the path of the guardrail plunging through the passenger window. Like a huge steel javelin it hit her between the eyes.

"Man, she's dead," said Henry. "Her head's caved in."

I leaned closer. The steel rail had crushed her lower forehead, cracked open a gaping hole between her eyes, sheared off the bridge of her nose and gouged out her right eye.

My legs trembled as I checked my watch and waited for the police. Night paled into dawn for twenty-five minutes before the first police car edged through the traffic. Two officers jumped out. One officer barely controlled himself while he examined the body.

"She's dead," he said, heading for his car.

A ranking officer pulled up and brought over his flashlight. I leaned down with him, following the light across the red mass of lacerated flesh and exposed bone that had been this young woman's face. Her right eye socket was all bloody tissue and pale shards of skull.

My gaze followed the light into the pink folds of her brain tissue. No blood pulsed anywhere. This officer went to fetch a body bag, leaving Henry and I alone with the two truckers.

"Let's just pray that her family be comforted," I told Henry. The truckers stood near as I began my soulish prayer. All at once the deep love of Jesus welled up in my heart. I began to think that this woman is somebody's daughter and perhaps she has children of her own. Maybe she had just dropped them off at a daycare center and now they don't know that mommy is dead. I thought of my own little sweet children hundreds of miles away.

Suddenly I stepped into the *secret place* of the Most High and His gentle love stilled my thoughts. I began to have a flash back to three days earlier. The compassion of Christ that He'd downloaded into the seat of my emotions that Thursday night revival service during Rosh Hashanah, now flowed out to this lost soul. I continued to pray compassionately in the Spirit. And suddenly she moved her head and begin to breath.

"She's alive!" I screamed!

The two truckers standing next to us gasped and then ran swiftly to their rigs and drove away. I moved closer. Blood pulsed from her wounds. The cold October air revealed mists of breath mixed with blood now venting from the splintered bridge of her nose. Henry and I rejoiced to see these gruesome signs of life. Blood pooled in her empty right eye socket.

I leaned down close and spoke words of life, urging her to receive the Lord. She moved her shattered jaw, trying to speak.

"Henry, maybe she doesn't know English," I said. "Lead her to Jesus in French." While he did, I thought of how surgeons can restore severed limbs today, so I searched the wreckage for her eyeball. I looked inside the car and on the ground, but didn't find it. I prayed again.

"O Lord, there's no use in You raising her from the dead and then having her face her children with a glass eye the rest of her life. Lord give her a new eye, and make sure it's a blue one!"

I didn't know why I prayed for a blue eye, since her one eye had remained closed. The policeman with stripes on his sleeve returned, unfolding a body bag.

"Don't do it," I said. "Look, she's breathing!"

He gasped and jumped back. Then I saw a veil of hardness come back on his face. "Well, she's not going to live anyway," he said, and unfolded the body bag.

"Don't you put that on her," I yelled. I'm a minister, and I'm telling you she won't be able to breath! Back off!"

"Yes sir," he said and backed down while bystanders strained to hear why I was yelling so loud.

0568

An ambulance and fire truck wailed through the traffic. The firemen cut her from the wreck, and her blood spilled over their equipment. We rejoiced knowing her heart still beat. The newspaper's color photograph of her being carried to the ambulance clearly showed blood brimming in her empty eye socket.[2]

That cold morning Henry and I drove on to the airport with our hearts fired by the love of Jesus. We laughed and wept with joy for how the Lord powerfully raised her from the dead. Though not usually used in the gift of tongues and interpretation, Henry suddenly burst out with a message and the interpretation. *"Sons, this is just the beginning of what I'm going to do in these last days. You have really seen nothing yet!"*

I flew back to my family in Saskatoon. Meanwhile, Henry called the police department to find out what hospital she was in.

"Oh, that woman's dead," they said. "Her family's being notified now."

"Dead? No, she was alive," Henry said.

"Sorry sir, she's dead." Click.

The following day, Henry's secretary called the police and described the incident. "Oh, you're the cult members," said the officer. "She's dead!" Click. In Quebec, if you're not Roman Catholic then you're labeled a cultist. But an hour later, a female officer called Henry's office.

"I'm a spirit filled Christian," she told him. "I can't tell you my name but the officer from the scene has been mocking you here at headquarters. The police report lists her as dead, and she was brought to a south shore hospital. God bless you." Click.

Henry rushed to the hospital and ran into the ICU. He didn't know the woman's name so he stopped the head nurse in the hall.

101

"We were at a car wreck yesterday," he said. "A blonde woman about thirty-five was killed. We prayed for her and she came back to life." The veteran head nurse began weeping.

"You're the one. Come with me." She led Henry into the waiting room and introduced him to the woman's family.

"Oh, you're her savior!" they said.

"No, I'm not her savior. Jesus is!"

The family explained how the police called them eight hours after the accident and told them to come identify their daughter's dead body, but instead, she was alive! "We don't know what's going on here," the family said, "but we're angry!"

They speculated that the first officer to reach the scene must have filed the police report listing her as killed. Henry told them all that happened, and the miracle deeply stirred them. The doors opened and the doctors appeared, smiling with encouragement.

"We've done a full MRI on your daughter," they said. "She had massive brain hemorrhaging, but it's subsiding now. And we were lucky to save her right eye."

"Right eye? What? There *was no* right eye!" said Henry.

"Oh, yes," the doctors said. "She arrived into the emergency unit and we had to repair damaged tissue around her face, but the eye itself was not injured."

Several weeks later I returned to Montreal and went to the hospital to visit Manon, the young woman. Her father was in the room and he told her in French who we were. Manon turned to face us, and she looked at me with two beautiful blue eyes. Overcome with weeping, I stepped out into the hall. I had seen the empty eye socket in the face of a dead woman. And now she was alive and looking at me with two blue eyes. God created a new eye for her during the trip in the ambulance and had definitely given her other unknown major overhauls in the process! She looked so different now! Hallelujah!!!

In French, Henry then told Manon's father that we were Christians and God raised his daughter from the dead and created a new eye for her. Suddenly the man's countenance became fiendish and a guttural voice rasped at us.

"You're not going to have her soul," he said in French. Henry told me later that the demon voice spoke a clearly different vocabulary than the man spoke and was infuriated about us not having her soul!

We later learned that he was building a lawsuit against the police, claiming his family suffered extreme anguish by hearing of their daughter's death when in fact she was alive. The two truck drivers were never found so we were the only witnesses. He made it impossible for us to visit her again. We concluded that he feared we would testify that she had been dead, and this would have hurt his case against the police. However, some members of the congregation were able to visit her, and we hear that she's doing well and now back home with her family. We are excited that one day God will fulfill all His purposes for Manon's life.

It's vital to understand that the miracle really took place Thursday night, three days before the accident. It was the compassion of Christ poured into me that night which later flowed out to raise that lost soul from the dead.

I did experience some sadness later, and confessed to the Lord how I'd pulled back from praying in total boldness because the policeman stood beside me. The young woman had scars from the reconstructive surgery that rebuilt her nose and jaw. I should have prayed that He would totally restore her and miraculously heal all her remaining scars.

We realize that we're just beginning to walk in this realm of His glory and have much to learn. Remember, flowing in the Secret Place with Abba is something that's more caught than taught.

Deep Freeze

God did not open the way for us to return to Montreal until January of 1998. We arrived during an historic ice storm. Quebec, and much of Canada, produces an extraordinary amount of hydroelectric power. Production is so prolific that they export electricity to the United States. That winter an unprecedented ice storm crippled this industry.

Thirty-story high electrical towers became sheathed in ice and toppled over. Dangerously long blackouts darkened whole areas of the cities and countryside, and curtailed industrial production. Many lives were lost and the nation was shaken. Canada's abundance of electrical power was a point of national pride, and now hundreds of thousands of Canadians stared out from darkened rooms at a world of ice.

During this emergency, our services were crowded with many coming to hear how God raised Manon from the dead. I always tell people that I'm just a guy from Oklahoma who learned to hear the gentle voice of the Lord and obey what He tells me. I exhort them to press into God, then rise up and do mighty exploits themselves.

"Truly, truly, I say to you, he who believes in Me, the works that I do, he will do also; and greater works than these he will do; because I go to the Father.

"Whatever you ask in My name, that will I do, so that the Father may be glorified in the Son.

"If you ask Me anything in My name, I will do it.

"If you love Me, you will keep My commandments."

John 14:12-15

Fat Tuesday

From the frigid North Country, we flew south to the Louisiana delta. Frank Bailey, pastor of Victory Fellowship in New Orleans, brought us down to hold meetings during Mardi Gras. Every year, this dynamic congregation joins with other street witnessing teams to bring the Gospel to the streets during this demonic celebration.

Tourism motivates New Orleans officials and business leaders to cordon off an "anything goes" portion of Bourbon Street. Tens of thousands of visitors join the city's pagan element in unleashing witchcraft, drunkenness and public debauchery, while unthinking families line the streets and TV commentators describe the fun.

In the early evening a few of us from the church walked over to Bourbon Street. The party had been roaring for several days already. The dedicated young workers knew what to expect, but I didn't realize we'd be walking through the gates of Sodom.

A cacophony of recorded music and live bands occupied the throng awaiting the lusty parade now forming up. We glimpsed the last day's deep darkness like a flash from the ancient scene of Sodom and Gomorrah.

We dared not look up as we walked past naked homosexual dancers performing unspeakable things on the streets without even the cover of darkness. I marveled how God's mercy still withholds His judgment from our nation, and tremble to imagine the fire that's coming.

Our group gathered in prayer and I blew God's warning trumpet ringing out over the revelers, preparing a way in the Spirit for the gospel witness. We left to prepare for the evening meeting. Later we felt compelled to wash the clothes we had worn into that atmosphere so charged with uncleanness and then learned of tornadoes dropping in the New Orleans area. I had ministered the day earlier on the "Tornado Vision" and had seen a young man give his life to Christ during the altar call. The following night I heard his father testify how his son went back home to his trailer park in Kissimmee, Florida only to find it totally destroyed by the largest system of killer tornadoes in Florida state history.[3] By God's grace he was spared because he chose to go to church that night in New Orleans instead of going back home to Florida. Praise God!

Later in the week, a group of those young workers came to one of our meetings and the team leader testified.

"The night you blew the shofar was the most powerful night of street ministry we've ever had at Mardi

Blowing a warning trumpet on Bourbon Street during Mardi Gras

Gras the last several years," one said. They told how individuals stopped at their curbside cross, broke into tears of repentance and met the Lord Jesus.

The following month we flew back to Canada, this time to the clear air and temperate climate of the beautiful city of Vancouver, British Columbia.

Chapter 7
Arise and Follow the Cloud

Then the Lord will create over the whole area of Mount Zion and over her assemblies a cloud by day, even smoke, and the brightness of a flaming fire by night; for over all the glory will be a canopy.

There will be a shelter to give shade from the heat by day, and refuge and protection from the storm and the rain.

Isaiah 4:5,6

In March of 1998, Pastor Ernie Culley brought us to Glad Tidings Assembly of Vancouver, British Columbia for a week of meetings. God graciously moved in our midst and we stayed for a second week. This gave me an opportunity to go out with the congregation's Lifeline Ministries. Every Monday night they bring a hot meal, clothing and groceries to Vancouver's homeless and poor. During the winter, Vancouver's temperate climate draws thousands of wandering drunks, ex-loggers and drug addicts, many of them homeless and infected with AIDS.

Members of the church spend most of Monday cooking up cauldrons of chili or stew. Later they load down their decrepit blue school bus with the hot meal, and hundreds of pounds of groceries and donated clothing, then drive to a certain empty lot in the city. They distribute the food and clothing while evangelism teams circulate among the homeless and the hopeless, offering them the good news. That Monday night we reached the normally empty lot and found it crowded by a production crew shooting the TV series, *The X-Files*.

Vancouver is called Hollywood North. The favorable exchange rate on the American dollar, and the abundance of skilled film professionals there, draw a growing volume of TV and film production work from Los Angeles to Vancouver.

Enormous generator trucks fouled the night air with diesel fumes as they pumped power along bundles of black cable running among the prop trucks, catering vans and mobile dressing rooms. Security guards and technicians worked or hung around, leaving little room for Lifeline Ministries. I was grieved to see God's people struggling to minister life from their old blue bus, while so much wealth and manpower served the darkness behind this show.

I believe that programs and movies like *The X-Files* are preparing the way for an alien invasion of demonic deception, displaying counterfeit signs and wonders that will ensnare millions of souls, hungry for the supernatural.

Pastor Culley describes what happened next.

"Toward the end of this frustrating night Scott stepped to one of our microphones. Something came over him and he stepped back. He said he was going to blow the shofar against *The X-Files*.

"You watch the papers," Scott declared. "*The X-Files* show is going to leave Vancouver. They're out of here and some of the actors will get saved!"

"Come on Scott," I thought. "You're talking about the second highest rated show on television." The Vancouver paper recently reported that the production company was pleased with their first five years of shooting here, and they planned to remain in Vancouver far into the future. The show has a huge following and there was nothing I could see that would change this.

*Scott blew the Shofar against the X-files resulting in their
sudden departure from Vancouver, BC*

Scott reared back and let fly with the shofar long and loud. Then we packed up and headed home. During the next few weeks the newspaper chronicled the amazing story. The day after the shofar blast, those running the show made a snap decision. Instead of remaining in Vancouver for years to come, they decided to move the entire production down to Los Angeles!

Our congregation was amazed when, a few weeks later, Grant Gladish came into our service. The young actor had just gotten his first big acting break in *The X-Files*. The Lord radically saved and delivered him. He

Scully, Mulder and Carter head for X-it

Popular locally made TV show will move to L.A. for next season

Stories by Mike Roberts
Staff Reporter and News Services

The truth is outta here.

It's official: The X-Files is bailing on Vancouver, its host city of five years. The most popular television series ever shot in Canada is moving to Los Angeles.

In a heartfelt address to the cast and crew Friday night in North Vancouver, X-Files creator and executive producer Chris Carter announced that the top-rated TV series would be leaving the Lower Mainland for Hollywood next season.

He thanked the City of Vancouver and the hundreds of Canadians who have helped make the series a success.

The X-Files publicist, Stephen Melnik, confirmed the FBI spooker is leaving town but added that an official announcement will not be made until later in the week.

"We are allowing Chris to talk to each of his cast and crew members this weekend

Reuter file photo

Vancouver newspaper headlines after the sounding of the shofar

gave half of his first *X-Files* paycheck to the church and the other half to Scott's ministry.

Before the week was out, we left a powerful service and took it to the streets again. Scott blew the shofar on the steps of Vancouver City Hall and prophesied against governmental corruption. Later, he blew it in front of the Jewish Community Center, praying we'd see the Spirit of God move upon the Jewish population of the city. Then Scott and his son Gideon joined my wife and me on some "drive-by shootings." We rolled past an abortion mill and then drove to an East Indian Seik Temple. Both times he blasted the trumpet for judgment against their works.

Since then, the Seik community has been prominent on the front pages of Vancouver papers. An intense power struggle erupted between two factions within the temple. Police entered the grounds and quelled the violence that had already claimed a man's life. And now for the first time hundreds of the Seik community have been coming to our services and accepting the gospel message of the Lord Jesus Christ and several prominent members of the Seik community have been healed! It is amazing!!!"

Once again during another street outreach with Glad Tidings Fellowship, the Lord stirred me up against the narcotics trade. We'd seen Mexico's most powerful drug lord die following the first shofar blast against the cartels, and in Delaware a popular crack cocaine den called "The Hole" had suddenly closed after we came against it.

Incensed with the way kids openly sold drugs in the Vancouver neighborhood close to where the church is located, I prayed against the drug dealers and blew the shofar. Later, we left the outreach service and found police checkpoints surrounding the neighborhood. Two hours after I sounded the shofar for judgment, the RCMP authorities nailed the West Coast's number one heroine dealer. The federal authorities described how they had trailed this Vietnamese man for five years from San Diego to his arrest that night in Vancouver, within hearing range of the shofar.

When God confirms the ministry of the shofar, the people are encouraged and excited to see what He will do in the future. But it's not always that way when we first arrive. Many pastors and congregations are a bit skeptical when we walk in with this twisted antelope horn, and they don't understand the Hebrew significance of the shofar. But then the glory of God rolls in to confirm His message with signs following.

An example of this occurred at World Harvest Church in Roswell, Georgia. Pastor Rodney Howard-Browne was unable to minister there, so Revival Ministries International referred us instead.

I set the shofar on the platform and taught the people how God moves in different ways when I blow the shofar over churches. Sometimes repentance hits the congregation, as it did atop Mount Royal. At other times the Lord ministers the Jubilee to His people, releasing blessings and financial breakthroughs. And then there are times when we're directed to leave the building and go to a specific location where the Spirit of God wants to demonstrate His power.

God later directed me to go to the congregation's new land. They had just broken ground, and put out their faith for the new building to go up debt-free. Pastor Mirck Hufton's wife, Linda, and some of their guests from South Africa were unfamiliar with this idea of blowing a horn over their property to release God's blessings. We're not surprised by these questions and we understand how new and unusual the shofar ministry is for many people. We later received a report from the Huftons, some of which follows.

A Pastor's Report

"Scott ministered at our church the week of July 5, 1998. Friday night after the meeting, he and about 40 of us went to our church property. We planned to begin building soon, but that day engineers told us we wouldn't be allowed to hook into the sewer system. This meant we would have to develop our own septic system, costing an additional $150,000 and taking up one-third of our property. The engineers told us that the city ordinances are never reversed, so we brought the problem to God.

After prayer and worship, Scott blew the shofar. It was around midnight and the sky was overcast. As we worshiped the Lord, someone called out. They pointed to a perfectly round hole forming in the clouds above us in the direction he'd blown the shofar. Through rings of layered clouds we looked upward through a clearing portal to the bright stars. We watched the clear circle expand outward, and in thirty minutes we stood amazed beneath the starry heavens!

During this time there was an awesome presence of the Lord, and we experienced a 'holy awe' in that place. Our children were very excited to witness a sign and a wonder in the sky. We remarked that it felt a little like being in the movie 'The Ten Commandments,' when the miracles took place.

Scott prophesied that we were witnessing an open heaven over our ministry and we would see many signs and wonders. One of those occurred just yesterday, August 13, 1998. The Fulton County director agreed to meet with my husband Mirck, who calmly pleaded our case and then waited. After a long silence, the director said that it was highly unusual, but he would give us permission to override the ordinance and hook into the present sewer system. We could do this not only for this new building, but for future buildings planned on that site.

The architect shared the news with the engineer who nearly fell out of his chair, and declared it was a miracle. Many times, he said they'd tried to get variances from the county and had always failed. With God all things are possible!"

New Exploits

Our scheduled ten days in Vancouver blossomed into four solid months of outstanding revival meetings. In May, Pastor Dave McGrew asked us to travel further north to minister at Chilliwack Christian Fellowship. The city of Chilliwack stands in the foothills above the Frazier Valley, dwarfed by the snow-covered Cascade Range. This settlement was a jumping off point for miners during the wild days of the 19th Century gold rush. God brought us there to minister to these hungry people, but also to give Dalit and me a pivotal word for our future ministry.

That Sunday morning I preached a message on knowing God intimately. Later, Pastor McGrew phoned me and said, "A friend called from Vancouver Airport. He's burning with a prophetic message that he must deliver here tonight. I told him to take the evening service."

"Sure," I said, "what's his name?"

"Dick Mills," Pastor McGrew said. "He's an old friend and he brings a very accurate word. He was just here two weeks ago, but must come back for one night. Something's up!"

The Sunday evening service began while Dick Mills drove nearly three hours to Chilliwack. When he walked into the meeting, we immediately turned things over to him. In his gentle off-hand manner this veteran of five decades of ministry began speaking prophetic words to various individuals. Dalit and I sat on the front row, eager to hear the burning word that compelled this 72 year-old brother to drive into the high country on a

Sunday night. He stopped, asked us who we were, and we told him.

"I need you to stand up," he said.

Suddenly his tone changed, becoming more intense. For five minutes he went on to deliver over Dalit and me the clear word the Lord had sent him there to speak.

"Isaiah 28:21," he began. "I'm putting together five translations for you. Everybody say to this couple, Good news!"

"Good news!" said the congregation, and they went on to echo his words as he continued to prophesy.

"Your prayer's been answered. The answer's on its way. It's an unusual answer and it's coming from an unexpected source. Let's go back over it again. Isaiah 28:21, this time from the New English Bible, The New Century Bible and the American Standard, 1901 version. The prayer's been heard. The answer's on its way. It is an unusual answer and it's coming from the most unexpected source. The bottom line is this: surprise!"

The people that do know their God shall be strong, and do exploits.
Daniel 11:32 (KJV)

The word 'know' used here has to do with an intimacy. We can know about Jesus by going to school and taking a class on comparative religions and getting a textbook on the history of Christianity. Or we can know Him intimately."

Knowing God intimately was the topic of my sermon that morning. At this point, Dick told an anecdote illustrating this intimacy.

"Stuart Hamlin was Billy Graham's first convert in LA, in 1949," Dick continued, "when Graham put up a tent on Hill Street. Hamlin had a radio show called "Stuart Hamlin's Lucky Stars." Later, he's in New York at the terminal. He's got his guitar and his amplifier and he's reading his Bible. A smart-mouthed New Yorker comes up and says, "Put away the book, cowboy, nobody's reading it anymore."

"Well I'm reading it," says Hamlin.

"Cowboy, the man you're reading about died two thousand years ago."

"That's funny," says Hamlin, "I just talked to Him a few minutes ago!"

"Everybody say this," said Dick. "Those that do know their God intimately will be strong. That word is *Nike*, which means to have spiritual clout, spiritual might that will pull down strongholds. Nike, victorious power and might! You're going to know the Lord intimately. You're going to have a prevailing spiritual clout and might to the pulling down of strongholds. Now I want to explain the word exploits. I need you to look straight at me."

Dalit and I focused our complete attention on him, riveted by the intensity of his ministry to us.

"Exploits are supernatural happenings that have not happened in antiquity. You can't go back into church history and locate them because they haven't happened yet. You can't find them on the contemporary scene. You can look all over the world but you won't find them anywhere today. Exploits are supernatural happenings that have not happened in the past. They are not happening now. But they're going to happen. And they're going to start with you!"

The congregation shouted, and Dalit and I were blown away. Then he laid hands on us, praying the Lord would seal this word, and we fell back.

Later I walked back to Pastor McGrew's office to speak with Dick. Reaching for the door I whispered, "God, I want to receive his fifty-four years of ministry anointing."

I opened the door. Dick looked up at me and said, "Young man, you can receive fifty-four years of anointing now. But I want what you have. I want your youthful vigor, now. Pray for me."

I reached out my hands to him and prayed, "Lord, give him a passion for Jesus and a spirit like Caleb."

"Yeah, Caleb, eighty-five years old," said Dick. "Yes, I receive it!"

This is a vital point in our whole story. Dick Mills said Dalit and I are carriers of something new that God wants to bring forth. From the beginning, *something new* has been a central theme of our ministry. Look once more at our ministry's key verse, Isaiah 43:18,19.

"Do not call to mind the former things, or ponder the things of the past.

"Behold, I will do something new, now it will spring forth; will you not be aware of it? I will even make a roadway in the wilderness, rivers in the desert."

Brother Dick defined the exploits that will come forth as supernatural happenings that have not taken place in antiquity. We can't look to the things of the past for understanding of these exploits because they have yet to appear on the earth.

119

Behold, I will do something new, now it will spring forth.

God challenged Dalit and I with this word, bringing us to a place of awe and increased responsibility before Him. Pastor Dave McGrew confirmed this by saying that he has known Dick Mills for many years and has never heard him prophecy like this before. Do you see, dear friend, how everything good flows out of intimacy with God in the Secret Place? Abba is waiting for you.

Milestones

It was after midnight, when Dalit and I drove past the mighty Cascade Range under a starry sky. We still felt stunned by the lingering power of the Spirit's words through Dick Mills, and the implications for our future ministry. Earlier events of our walk with God now passed like milestones before us.

I recalled that night in Tulsa, eleven years ago, when I cried out to God, and the Holy Spirit spoke through me, promising a release of great power, glory and finances to the Church in the last days. The sign confirming this word was the Great Tulsa Flood of '87. Later that same night, God promised that disgraced TV Evangelist Jim Bakker would be restored one day. Anyone who experiences the ministry of this broken servant, or reads his excellent book, *"I Was Wrong,"* knows that Jim Bakker is now restored. Expectation surged through us in the car as we longed to see the fulfillment of God's promised power, glory and finances flowing through the Church.

We recalled our first shofar exploit at Lubavitch World Headquarters, and how envoys from around the globe mourned the man who did not rise up as Messiah.

Wall Street came before us next, and we marvelled how high the stock market had risen since we blew the shofar and when the great bull market would come crashing down as the Lord had said. We thought of the *The X-Files,* entrenched in Vancouver, then suddenly leaving town. Dalit and I talked about the many churches where the Jubilee trumpet released blessings and changed lives and families forever. I saw the blue eyes of Manon, who had died and was now alive. And now, with this night's prophetic word ringing in our souls, we looked at one another. There's more? Something new! Let's go for it!

Just then, Dalit and I remembered something that happened in January of '95, while we were still in Brooklyn. The children and I had driven to Kennedy Airport to meet Dalit's return flight. I'd sent her to Rodney Howard-Browne's Winter Campmeeting in Lakeland, Florida. Dalit got into the car.

"Mommy, look at you," the kids said.

The glory of God shone on her face.

"I'm not going back to religion," she said. "Never!"

The glory increased and came upon me. I reached for the gear shift and the windshield disappeared, replaced by a vision. I saw a color bar graph which charted the spiritual heights of various well-known ministries. On the graph a line of glory separated the natural realm below from the supernatural realm above. One ministry, which I knew preached salvation and the Baptism of the Holy Spirit, stopped just above the glory line. A popular Evangelical ministry rose near the line but never crossed it. A famous healing and miracle ministry rose well above the line, then stopped. I understood that this ministry was satisfied with their miracles, and had no hunger for more of God.

"I'm going all the way," I said. "I won't stop."

Right then I resolved to always press on into more of God. The vision vanished and we drove away. The following month we left the Brooklyn congregation, incorporated Rivers in the Desert International, and began traveling. Soon after this, Dalit was given a vision, perhaps a visitation, while she slept. This is how she describes it.

Dalit's Dream

I see a lady sitting in the water, drowning men with her hand, one after another. This Jezebel spirit chases me carrying a long needle which she tries to plunge into my heart. I reach a sort of bus or boat, and once inside with other believers, I know I'm safe. A voice tells me that it's not time yet to go to Israel, because of the deadly mines in the waters there.

Then it's night and I'm looking at New York City. Lightning flashes from east to west, beyond the tall buildings. The verse from Matthew 24:27 comes to me.

For just as the lightning comes from the east and flashes even to the west, so will the coming of the Son of Man be.

Suddenly, the city lights up like the dawn. An angel with a trumpet flies over declaring, "Jesus is coming! Jesus is coming!"

Next I see a rider atop a powerful white horse. To my right stand many famous Christian ministers and singers. A second angel comes flying this way, and I assume he's headed toward those prominent people, but he comes to me. We shake hands.

"I'm pleased with you," he says. *"Prepare ye the way of the Lord!"*

The angel goes on to speak about my relationship with Scott, and tells me to be more patient with my children. Then, in my dream, I begin singing in the spirit.

I woke up, still singing. Since this dream, I've sung more and more in the spirit, both alone and during our meetings. Although I'm not a trained singer, God uses my voice in exhorting people to rise up and move forward. I hope this encourages others to sing out with their own spontaneous songs of worship to the Lord.

Song of the Lord

During the long months on the road, Dalit cared for and schooled our four children in hotel rooms. To follow the moving of the Holy Spirit, we've had to adjust to restaurant food, strange hours and unexpected changes in our plans, such as packing for a ten-day trip that became a sudden four-month series of revival meetings.

In June of 1998, we ministered in another Vancouver congregation. God had already brought this congregation into a place of deep worship. Our "Arise" recording (see the last page for more information) features segments of the spontaneous worship from these June meetings, some of which lasted into the early morning hours. This music was totally unrehearsed and all the words, melodies, chords, and rhythms were choreographed by the Holy Spirit as we and the music teams were spontaneously worshipping the Lord. The intensity of the glory of God and prophetic words that followed the blasts of the shofar signaled to all that were present, that the Holy Spirit is doing something so new and unparalleled, that now it is the time for us all to "Arise and Shine!" We saw whole families weep together in repentance and individuals remain prostrate on the floor until the next day. During these meetings one night I saw Jesus walk into the sanctuary.

In silhouette form, the Lord walked up and down the aisles carrying a horn filled with oil. I understood that He was going throughout the earth, visiting all the extended revival meetings, searching for the sons of Jesse. He passed by those believers who had jumped on the bandwagon and had come to revival for the excitement and the blessings. Jesus paused and poured fresh oil of the Spirit only upon those few with hearts after God like David, who worshiped with spontaneous songs from the depth of their being. All they want to do is worship and please God. From among these, the cream of the crop, He is commissioning new leaders for the next wave of His power and glory which will cover the earth as the waters cover the sea.

Shouting

According to The Theological Wordbook of the Old Testament, the Hebrew word *"rinna" (to cry out, shout for joy)* is so frequently employed in the Psaltery of ancient Israel that it indicates decisively that the highest mood of Old Testament religion was joy. However, it is found most often only translated as "singing" in the King James Version. But this actual Hebrew word describes something very different than our modern, Western singing. Jubilant shouting or ringing cries of joy are actually a more accurate representation of this Hebrew word when it was incorporated in the worship services and festive gatherings of ancient Israel.[1]

This *rinnah*, when incorporated in revival services launches people into higher realms of the Spirit. There's a place in the Holy Spirit where God's worshipping people hear a sound coming from heaven from God Himself singing or responding in ringing cries of joy. Soon we'll be hearing more and more about this sound from heaven.

"The LORD your God is in your midst, a victorious warrior. He will exult over you with joy, He will be quiet in His love, He will rejoice over you with shouts of joy."

Zephaniah 3:17

These verses show God rejoicing over His people with *rinnah*, ringing cries and shouts of joy. Talk about a sound from heaven that will shake and startle the enemies camp! No wonder the demons tremble in terror at the mere mention of His name!

Ephesians 5:18,19 describes some of the reasons for, and the fruit of, being filled with the Spirit.

And do not get drunk with wine, for that is dissipation, but be filled with the Spirit,

speaking to one another in psalms and hymns and spiritual songs, singing and making melody with your heart to the Lord.

I said all this to say, people with hearing hearts will increasingly move on from the usual singing of the usual songs, and the Western worship industry will not be able to market this new sound from heaven. Not that there's anything wrong with currently recorded worship music. But there's a particular sound accompanying every move of God. And God will use those with hearts like David to release new sounds and dimensions of power and glory through jubilant, shouting, whirling, trumpeting explosions of worship as we are filled with His Spirit! Remember the woman at the well in John chapter four was looking for water; but Jesus said He would give her living water that would cause her to enter a place of being a true worshipper. This is the people Abba seeks to be His worshippers — River people! This is the purpose of Rivers in the Desert prophecy from Isaiah 43:18-21, to cause His people to have drink and so they can show forth His highest praise! This is the cloud that is moving in the current hour.

Flashfloods.com

Back home in Tampa, we rested, then set to work upgrading our ministry outreach with the help of a talented webmaster, Tony Reynolds.

Located on our new website of *www.flashfloods.com* is an example of this new spontaneous prophetic music that recently has been emerging in the extended revival meetings where the Holy Spirit is allowed to flow freely and unrestricted. And combined with the blasts of the shofar, it is really powerful and refreshing music to listen constantly to in your home or automobile.

In July of '98, while working on this book and preparing for the birth of Yotam, our fifth child, Pastor Frank Bailey brought me back to New Orleans. He knows Dick Mills very well, so I asked Pastor Bailey to listen to the word spoken over us in Chilliwack.

"I've known Dick Mills for twenty years," he said. "He has one of the surest prophetic words I know of, and I've never heard him prophecy like this."

Later, during the meeting, Pastor Bailey suddenly jumped up and came forward.

"Scott, the Lord just told me to pray over you, now. For the beginning of God's word through Dick Mills to begin in your ministry. You can't make it happen. You just have to wait." Oh those words *"wait"* brought me back again to the old synagogue building in Brooklyn, New York, where I first learned to wait quietly on the still small voice of Abba. And he thrust us out into the signs and wonders ministry based on His prophetic word through Rodney Howard-Browne. Now I am excitedly facing an even greater prophetic word from Abba through Dick Mills and the rules still cannot be forced or changed. I must again seek Him diligently and still myself as I did before in May of 1994 (see chapter 1).

Minutes later, after silently pondering these past victories, God prompted me to blow the shofar. I obeyed, having no idea that the first answer to Frank Bailey's prayer would come so soon. A local pastor from Louisiana had driven over for the meeting. The following is taken from his letter of August 10, 1998, describing what he experienced.

"My wife and I were raised in pastor's homes, and we've been around the supernatural all our lives! But what happened to me on the night of July 27 was a very different level of His presence. The service began with the Victory Fellowship team leading us in praise and worship for about an hour. The level of God's glory seemed to rise with each song, and I began to sense God's presence in very tangible ways. Then I heard the sound of Scott's shofar.

Waves of sound hit me and I suddenly felt a force lift me upward. It's hard to explain, but the sound of the shofar lifted me upward. I expected to leave my body at any moment. I believe I know now what it will feel like to be raptured when Jesus returns for His bride.

When the shofar sounded again, my consciousness was no longer in the auditorium, but out in the wilderness. In daylight I stood looking out from the entrance of a tent. All around me stood thousands of tents, arranged in four directions, surrounding the tabernacle of Moses.

The sound of the shofar was like a living sound, something I'd never experienced before. The shofar "spoke" to me by the force of the sound hitting me. I felt the shofar say, *"Arise and follow the cloud. You have camped long enough and the cloud is moving. Follow the cloud to a new place."*

"Excitement filled me as I, and the entire camp, watched the cloud of God's glory move forward. I recall thinking how strange it was to be standing on a desert floor some thousands of years ago while, at the same time, standing on the floor of Victory Fellowship. The desert seemed more real. The shofar felt like the voice of God drawing me upwards into His presence.

I believe the Lord gave me this experience to focus my vision on Him, and to prepare me for the changes about to happen in our congregation and in His Church worldwide. A fresh, completely different move of the Spirit is at the door.

Whenever I recall how I felt and what I sensed in the Spirit during this vision, there's a desire in me to surrender more of my life to Jesus, and allow the Holy Ghost to prepare me to house a greater measure of His glory. For those Christians who will allow the presence of God to work deeply in their lives, the Lord is about to give an unprecedented measure of His glory!"

The Cloud Is Now Moving

"Moses My servant is dead; now therefore arise, cross this Jordan, you and all this people, to the land which I am giving...."

Joshua 1:2

Recently while in extended revival meetings again in Canada, the Spirit of God whispered to me that a "Changing of the Guard" was beginning in North America among His current spiritual leaders and that we would see a rapid succession of the current guards that have pioneered before us, going home to heaven and entering into their eternal rewards. A sudden departure of these spiritual leaders would stun the Christian community world-wide and thus signaling a new course and direction the Holy Spirit was taking us into. The stepping up of a new Joshua generation was now beginning, and it was time to forget the past and boldly forge out into the new awakening that is on the horizon!

By faith, I began to boldly minister this message, coupled with the shofar blasts, to alert the believers in these revival meetings that now is the time to "Arise and Shine" because something new is happening with the baton of leadership in the Church. After the evening service, the pastor of this particular fellowship quickly approached me and said he must talk with me privately since he had just received tragic news from a friend in Central America. As the leaders and myself sat in his office, he began to describe in detail the conversation he had with this missionary who had survived a horrendous plane crash that had killed the key leaders of a wonderful missionary organization.

We all began to weep as we were told the names of these leaders and then the pastor continued to say that their church had even planned to send a short term missions team to that organization in Central America but at the last moment, the Holy Spirit told them to cancel the trip. Our weeping turned into joy at the mercy of God, but we still remained bewildered on how such powerful missionary leaders died so tragically in the prime of life.

The following week of revival services however, flushed out all lingering confusion as powerful appearances of the glory of God characterized those services with several eyewitness accounts of people seeing angels walk through the services! The electrifying presence of God had charged the air so powerfully that week that I can still feel it as I write the final stages of this book. Glory to God!

The following week, we traveled to another church for revival services, and the anointing came again to sound the shofar and to preach the message "The Changing of the Guard." The following day the pastor received a sudden phone call from a very close family who's father had just died a few hours earlier. The pastor described in detail to us how he had worked closely with this dear man of God for many years who had started a wonderful Christian book publishing company and had at one time overseen over 1500 churches under his organization. Again I began to have a flashback from the week before and then plowed through the emotional sorrow of another great man of God going home. The feeling of the shortness of the hour then caused the remainder of the revival services that week to be punctuated with many messages of holiness and purity of heart.

The following week we again traveled to another church and on a Thursday night the powerful anointing returned again to sound the alarm and proclaim "The Changing of the Guard." After the service concluded with wonderful spontaneous worship, the pastor was leaving the parking lot and then suddenly pulled his car around and sped back to us and reported that he had

just heard on the radio that the most prominent evangelist in their province for the last 25 years had just suddenly died that night during the meeting! Dalit and I
were stunned as well as the entire congregation, and we
decided urgently to re-examine our own personal lives
and make any necessary changes the Holy Spirit showed
us so we could finish the race.

We then drove 2600 miles cross-country with our
five little children through several ice storms and even
slamming into a deer at 60 mph to make it in time for
revival services in Atlanta, Georgia. The message and
the anointing resurfaced again to blow the shofar and
announce "The Changing of the Guard." I then was told
the following day that one of the great Christian pastors
of our time was just admitted to the hospital with seri-
ous complications. We again were stunned and told the
congregation that we were scheduled to be next in the
city of Houston, Texas in the area where this wonderful
man of God pastored. The enormity and complexity of
how our revival meetings could coincide with all these
events was mind-boggling!

We arrived later in Houston just a few days after his
glorious home going and began revival meetings. A
very strong presence of the glory of God hovered in
these meetings with some of them lasting until four in
the morning. Many of the believers that have been
touched by this man's loving ministry were so encouraged to hear all the messages God placed on our hearts
during these meetings. We all enthusiastically embraced
the new door of responsibility that is required of us who
are running with the message of revival and the new
thing the Holy Spirit is doing world-wide.

Then again, suddenly some local Houston ministers and myself were up at 3 a.m. basking in the glory of God after a service and began to hear the Holy Spirit signaling still yet another great man of God was about to go home to his reward. We all sat there humbled and stunned at the rapid succession of what already had happened. Then the following week, we received the report that this wonderful man of God was also hospitalized and at the writing of this final chapter of this book, we are in prayer for his full recovery and powerful ministry to be extended by the grace of Abba Father.

Dear friends, I have been deeply stirred by the lateness of the hour and the sudden passing of these great men of God with such rapid succession. The Holy Spirit is alerting all of us that the cloud is moving, and we must enter into these men's labors, pick up the baton, and sprint ahead into the great harvest that is now awaiting us here on planet earth. These powerful men and women of God that have led us to the current camps we are now in are passing over to the other side and entering into their eternal rewards. We will never in this life fully understand the secret things of the Father and why certain things have happened the way they have, but we will remember the wonderful impartations of love and the anointings these pioneers have graced the world with. Yes, we will miss them greatly as we continue to read their writings and watch their images from video tape. Yet, I believe a greater emotion than we have yet to experience is now about to boil from within our hearts.

That greater emotion will be the courageous drive to grasp tightly in our hands their passing baton and see them smile as we now turn to sprint the final leg of this great race of faith. They have completed their race and now are waiting with the Master Himself at the finish line to see Him embrace our smiling faces.

C'mon dear brothers and sisters, let's run with the vision and finish this race of the intimate knowledge of the glory of the Lord filling the earth as the waters have total coverage over the sea!!!

Then the Lord answered me and said, "Record the vision and inscribe it on tablets, that the one who reads it may run.

"For the vision is yet for the appointed time; it hastens toward the goal and it will not fail. Though it tarries, wait for it; for it will certainly come, it will not delay.

"Behold, as for the proud one, His soul is not right within him; but the righteous will live by his faith.

"For the earth will be filled with the knowledge of the glory of the Lord, as the waters cover the sea."

Habakkuk 2:2-4,14

Epilogue

Dear friends we have now entered the thresholds of an unparalleled awakening that is visiting our civilization. Now is the time to awaken from sleep and let the glory of Christ shine upon us. It is time to consider how we walk and conduct ourselves during our brief sojournings on this planet. We must redeem the time for the days are evil and the trumpet is sounding a very distinct clarion call. To not do this is to be utterly foolish and self-willed. The way to avoid being foolish and complacent is to allow ourselves to be continually and habitually filled with the Holy Spirit (study Ephesians 5:7-21).

We have decided to conclude this book at the very moment of the stillness before the storm of tornadoes approaches. We want you as the reader to take to heart the teachings and testimonies of this book and find a place where you can get alone and be quiet with the Holy Spirit. Do it now and don't delay!

Endeavor with all your strength and desire to come away from the electronic entertainments of this age and its distracting amusements and allow His still presence to settle in and around your heart and mind. Don't be in a rush to leave this Secret Place of fellowship when you suddenly discover it. It is the place of Psalms 91 protection and provision. It is the place of joy unspeakable and glorious pleasures forevermore.

It is the place of activation of the prophecies over your life that have been in a holding pattern of seemingly perpetual unfulfillment. It will wonderfully change your family, your marriage, your business and everything you endeavor to do for Him! As you hear His gentle whisper from the secret place, He too will launch you into exciting spontaneous signs and wonders for the harvest of lost souls.

Constantly remind yourself that this is the best investment of your time in this current hour of preparation and separation from the spirit of this age. The cloud is moving into the new thing. Let's be wise and do His will and thus have sufficient oil to enter into the wedding feast as a wise virgin, hearing the Master say:

"…'Well done, good and faithful slave. You were faithful with a few things, I will put you in charge of many things; enter into the joy of your master.'"

Matthew 25:23

Stay tuned. As God unfolds the new thing He is doing in the earth, we will bring you continuing testimonies in the next upcoming sequel to *"Gentle Whisper of the Secret Place."*

Notes

Chapter 1 — The Secret Place

[1] R. Laird Harris, Gleason L. Archer, Bruce K. Waltke, *Theological Wordbook of the Old Testament* (Chicago: Moody Press, 1980), Vol. 2, p. 917.

[2] Harris, Archer, Waltke, Vol. 2, p. 916.

[3] Harris, Archer, Waltke, Vol. 1, pp. 193, 195.

[4] Harris, Archer, Waltke, Vol. 2, p. 938.

[5] Harris, Archer, Waltke, Vol. 1, p. 193.

[6] *New York Daily News*, June 13, 1994, p. 4.

[7] *The Jewish Press*, Vol. XLIV No. 24, Week of June 17-June 23, 1994, p. 1.

[8] *New York Daily News*, June 13, 1994, p. 5.

[9] *The Jewish Press*, Vol. XLIV No. 24, Week of June 17-June 23, 1994, p. 1.

[10] *The Jewish Press*, June 17-June 23, 1994 p. 100.

[11] *Logos Library System for Microsoft*, version 2.1c (Washington: Logos Research Systems Inc.,1998), "Gethsemane."

Chapter 2 — From Tulsa to Leningrad

[1] *The Jerusalem Post International Edition*, No. 1623, December 14, 1991, p. 1.

[2] *The Jerusalem Post International Edition*, February 15, 1992, p. 1.

[3] *The Jerusalem Post International Edition*, February 15, 1992, p. 11.

[4] Harris, Archer, Waltke, Vol. 2, p. 938.

Chapter 3 — Tornado Vision

[1] *USA Today*, Friday February 14, 1997, p. 1.

[2] *USA Today*, Tuesday February 2, 1999, p. 3.

[3]   *The News Journal*, Wilmington, DE., Thursday April 4, 1996, p. 1.

[4]   *All Politics*, http:\\allpolitics.com\1998\08\06\lewinsky\, Thursday, August 6, 1998, p. 1.

Chapter 4 — Jubilee

[1]   Harris, Archer, Waltke Vol. 1, pp. 358, 359.

Chapter 5 — Revival in Canada

[1]   *The Jerusalem Post Internet Edition*, Friday Jan. 17, 1997, www.jpost.com, p.1.

[2]   *Montreal Gazette*, Monday July 7, 1997.

Chapter 6 — Behold, I Do Something New

[1]   *The Jerusalem Post Internet Edition*, Sunday Oct 19, 1997, www.jpost.com, p.1-3.

[2]   *Le Journal De Montreal*, Monday October 6, 1997, p.12.

[3]   *The Times-Picayune*, Tuesday February 24, 1998, p.1.

Chapter 7 — Arise and Follow the Cloud

[1]   Harris, Archer, Waltke, Vol. 2, p. 851.

Scott M. Holtz is the President and Founder of Rivers in the Desert International. Since 1995, he and his wife Dalit have been traveling extensively in North America conducting revival meetings with powerful visitations of the Glory of God in many of the services. These types of meetings are to get the believers out of the pews and into the streets with the good news of the gospel.

Deborah

Scott and Dalit are both from Jewish backgrounds. Dalit served in an elite Commando unit in the Israeli Defense Forces. Scott was raised in Tulsa, Oklahoma and graduated from Oral Roberts University. (They really count all this biographical achievement info as "rubbish" and would much rather boast about their weaknesses that the power of Messiah would come and enshrine itself in a greater measure in their earthly tabernacles [II Corinthians 12:9]. Hallelujah!)

Yael

Together with their five children they have received a commission from God to run swiftly throughout the nations and herald forth the message that He is presently doing something so unprecedented, unparalleled, and unpredictable that it will utterly astonish and perplex our entire civilization. To accomplish this God has given them unique messages that infuse faith, change, and excitement into His people. These messages rekindle believers into fervency for Jesus and is accompanied by powerful signs and wonders of Heavenly origin.

Ronit

Scott and Dalit presently reside near Tampa, Florida with their five beautiful children (Gidon, Deborah, Yael, Ronit and Yotam).

Gidon & Yotam

To receive Scott Holtz Ministries free bimonthly
newsletter, please write to:

Rivers in the Desert International

P.O. Box 1799

Valrico, FL 33595

or visit our website at: www.flashfloods.com

Prayer of Salvation

Perhaps you have read some of the incredible events that are told in this book and are thinking about where you would go and spend eternity if you died tonight. The Word of God says, "for all have sinned and fall short of the glory of God" (Romans 3:23). That means, in the current state which you are living in, you cannot make it to heaven unless you are "born anew" or "born from above." To be born from above, you must turn from your own selfish ways and accept the sacrifice for your sins through the gift of God's Son, the Lord Jesus the Messiah. This surrender to the free gift of God's love will cause your heart to be supernaturally made new, and then you will be able to live in a way pleasing to your new Heavenly Father. We would love to have the great privilege of praying with you and leading you to a new relationship with Him. The Bible says that if any man or woman will call upon the name of the Lord, they will be saved (Romans 10:13).

Go ahead now and pray this prayer with me. Say, *"Father, I ask you in the name of your Son Jesus to forgive me of my sins. The Bible says if anybody will call upon your Name, he or she would be saved. I'm calling today, Lord. Save me. Forgive me. Cleanse me. Take all of my sins and rebellious ways and cast them into the sea of forgetfulness. Throw them as far as the East is from the West, never to be remembered again. I believe in my heart that you raised Jesus from the dead. And I now say with my mouth, 'Jesus be my Lord!' Father, I'm running home to you now. In the name of your Son Jesus, I pray, Amen."*

If you prayed that prayer, we would like to welcome you to the family of God today! If you want to tell us about your life changing decision and want more information on how we can help you, just contact us with the information provided below. God Bless you! We love you!

NEW ADDRESS!!

Rivers In The Desert International
P.O. Box 2788
Alpharetta, GA 30023-2788
(770) 777-0143
Website: www.flashfloods.com
E-mail: sh@flashfloods.com